THE

Everlasting Love

To Kim & Skye,
May God bless
your marriage with
everlasting joy!

Karee Santos

"What Dr. Manny and Karee Santos have done with *The Four Keys to Everlasting Love* is to create a resource that we all need. Yes, all of us. Whether you're single and contemplating marriage, newlywed or an old hand at vows, priest or catechist, this book has something for you. What you're holding in your hands is a book that's going to become an instant, classic, go-to resource for parishes, spiritual leaders, and anyone who cares about the future of Catholic marriage."

Sarah Reinhard
Catholic author, speaker, and blogger

"In *The Four Keys to Everlasting Love*, you will meet two remarkable people who have experienced authentic love, having embraced joy and sorrow alike. Practical yet spiritually rich, this book is the fruit of Manny's private practice as a counselor to couples in crisis and of their ministry together in marriage preparation. While reading it you will discover, as the Santoses have discovered, that just as Jesus turned water into wine at the wedding feast of Cana, he 'restores the wine' in the lives of every couple who invite him to their marriage."

From the foreword by **Christopher West**
Author of *Good News about Sex and Marriage*

"I marvel at the evangelizing power of the family! Fearlessly sharing their own marital and family struggles, Karee and Manny show how every family can reach the alluring ideal to which God calls them, drawing others to heaven in the process. Their many easy and practical suggestions are spot on!"

Rev. John R. Waiss
Pastor and author of *Couples in Love*

"Whether engaged or long married, Catholic couples will fall in love again as they implement these simple but powerful strategies for creating a lifetime of mutual joy. *The Four Keys to Everlasting Love* unpacks the secrets of genuine togetherness through personal witness, case studies, the writings of the Church, and superb practical recommendations. Not to be missed!"

Lisa Mladinich
Author of the Be an Amazing Catechist series

"In my experience as a Catholic relationship book junkie, this is my first encounter with a book that spans every season of marriage, from engagement to young family life and beyond. Karee and Manny Santos offer something rare: practical, livable, and holy ways for couples to live out their wedding vows in a complete gift of self—in everything from work to money to holidays and hospitality. Looking to scripture, the saints, and St. John Paul II's theology of the body, their wisdom, born of many years together in sickness and in health, does more than just present a road map for the shared life between a husband and wife and their family. *The Four Keys to Everlasting Love* calls spouses to a true engagement (ahem!) and communion with the Church and the world, one that authentically fosters a 'civilization of love.' This book truly is an invitation to heroic virtue, fully alive in pursuit of God's glory, with your spouse by your side."

Stephanie Calis
Catholic blogger and author of
Invited: The Ultimate Catholic Wedding Planner

THE FOUR KEYS TO
Everlasting Love

How Your

Catholic Marriage

Can Bring You

Joy for a Lifetime

KAREE SANTOS AND
MANUEL P. SANTOS, MD

AVE MARIA PRESS AVE Notre Dame, Indiana

Nihil Obstat: Reverend Nicholas Zientarski, S.T.D.
                    Censor Librorum
Imprimatur: Most Reverend William Murphy, S.T.D., L.H.D.
                    Bishop of Rockville Centre
Given at Rockville Centre, New York, October 19, 2015

Founded in 1865, Ave Maria Press is a ministry of the United States Province of Holy Cross.

www.avemariapress.com

Paperback: ISBN-13 978-1-59471-603-4

E-book: ISBN-13 978-1-59471-604-1

Cover image © stocksy.com, thinkstock.com.

Cover and text design by Katherine Coleman.

Printed and bound in the United States of America.

Library of Congress Cataloging-in-Publication Data
Names: Santos, Karee.
Title: The four keys to everlasting love : how your Catholic marriage can bring you joy for a lifetime / Karee Santos and Manuel P. Santos, MD.
Description: Notre Dame : Ave Maria Press, 2016. | Includes bibliographical references and index.
Identifiers: LCCN 2015039389 | ISBN 9781594716034 (pbk. : alk. paper) | ISBN
    9781594716041 (e-book : alk. paper)
Subjects: LCSH: Marriage--Religious aspects--Catholic Church. | Catholic Church--Doctrines.
Classification: LCC BX2250 .S237 2016 | DDC 248.8/44088282--dc23
LC record available at http://lccn.loc.gov/2015039389

To our parents,

who have celebrated their

golden wedding anniversaries,

for showing us how it's done

Contents

Foreword

Whether you're married or single, when someone starts talking about "keys" in marriage it's only a matter of time before someone starts joking about the "old ball and chain"—as though marriage marks the end of a person's freedom.

The truth is that marriage is a tremendous and beautiful *use* of one's freedom. "Freedom exists for the sake of love," as St. John Paul II wrote in his marvelous work *Love and Responsibility*. "If freedom is not . . . taken advantage of by love it becomes a negative thing and gives human beings a feeling of emptiness." Man "longs for love more than for freedom—freedom is the means and love is the end" (*LR*, 135–136).

The question we must ask however is, what is love? While there are a lot of counterfeit loves on the market, Christ proclaims himself the "way, the truth, and the life," leading us ever closer to real love as we follow him faithfully. This is love: that we learn how to lay down our lives as Christ has done for his Bride, the Church. Marriage is a sacrament precisely because it is meant to be a living image and participation in the love of Christ and the Church. But how does Christ love?

Christ's love seems distinguishable by four particular qualities. First, Christ loves *freely* ("No one takes [my life] from me, but I lay it down of my own accord" [Jn 10:18]). Second, he loves *totally*—without reservation, condition, or selfish calculation ("He loved them to the end" [Jn 13:1]). Third, he loves *faithfully* ("I am with you always" [Mt 28:20]). And fourth, he loves *fruitfully* ("I came that they may have life" [Jn 10:10]). If we are to avoid the pitfalls of counterfeit love and live marriage to the full, we must strive to express the same free, total, faithful, fruitful love that Christ expresses.

It is precisely this to which a bride and groom commit themselves at the altar. The priest or deacon asks them, "Have you come here *freely* and *without reservation* to give yourselves to each other in marriage? Do you promise to be *faithful* all the days of your lives? Do you promise to *receive children* lovingly from God?" Their wholehearted "yes" to each of these questions binds the couple in a life-long sacramental union, leading them along a pathway of loving fidelity that will guide them heavenward.

Marriage, we all know, is not easy. In certain seasons of married life, the struggles, conflicts, tensions, sorrows, and sufferings can seem to rob us of the joy we antici-pated when we committed to love one another freely, totally, faithfully, and fruitfully at the altar. Embracing these sufferings is also part of learning to "love as Christ loves." And precisely in and through these sufferings, we find the path to becoming the men and women we are created to be.

In *The Four Keys to Everlasting Love*, you will meet Karee and Dr. Manuel (Manny) Santos, two remarkable people who have experienced authentic love, having embraced joy and sorrow alike. Practical yet spiritually rich, this book is the fruit of his private practice as a coun-selor to couples in crisis and of their ministry together in marriage preparation. While reading it you will discover, as the Santoses have discovered, that just as Jesus turned water into wine at the wedding feast of Cana, so too does he "restore the wine" in the lives of every couple who invite him to their marriage. Throughout scripture, wine is a symbol of divine love. When the married couple at Cana ran out of wine, it's an indication of the loss of God's love in the human heart that happened with original sin. *That* is where all the tension and difficulties of marriage begin. But the good news—the "gospel of marriage"—is that Christ has restored the wine to married life in super-abundance . . . and through this book he invites us to drink up!

That's what the Santoses invite us to do as well. So pour yourself a glass of wine, settle in for a quiet read, and spend some time just the two of you rediscovering for yourselves the goodness and joy that may be found in learning to love as Christ loves.

Christopher West
Author of *Good News about Sex and Marriage*

Introduction

"And they lived happily ever after." Wouldn't you like that to be the story of your marriage, the story of your life? God wants to give that life to you. His love for you is unmatched in power, intensity, depth, and tenderness. If you want to learn how to love and be loved forever, there is no greater teacher than the love of Jesus Christ.

God's love for you is faithful. He has said, "I will not leave you" (Jn 14:18). He has sworn never to forsake you (Dt 31:6). He will stay with you always, even to the end of the world (Mt 28:20).

God's love for you is free. He has invited you, even you with nothing to give him, to feast at the banquet of his love, to eat and drink your fill "without money and without price" (Is 55:1).

God's love for you is fruitful. You will reap a harvest of eternal life if you do not give up or grow weary in doing what is right (Gal 6:9). God's love will lead you to all that is right and true (Eph 5:9), and it will show itself in the good works that you do (Col 1:10).

God's love for you is total. He will refresh you when you are tired and weary (Jer 31:25), he will heal your heart when it is broken (Is 61:1), he will take away your sickness (Dt 7:15), and he will wipe away every tear from your eyes (Rv 21:3–4). He would joyfully and willingly die for you. In fact, he has already died for you.

God wants us to receive his faithful, free, fruitful, and total love, and then share it with one another. Jesus didn't say only to love your neighbor as yourself. He said "love one another as I have loved you" (Jn 15:12). Like Jesus, we can love with firm commitment and intense loyalty. We can love despite the misunderstandings, the pettiness, the hurts, and the betrayals. What do we call this love that knows no bounds? It is spousal love, as St. John Paul II explained it. It is the love of Christ the Bridegroom for his people—his Bride, the Church.

The bad news is that you cannot achieve this perfection of spousal love on your own. The good news is you don't have to. Jesus freely offers showers of graces to couples united in the Sacrament of Matrimony. He wants your marriage to be a sign—a sacrament—of his divine spousal love for the world.

Jesus treasured marriage so much that he performed his first miracle at a wedding—the wedding at Cana, where he turned water into wine (see Jn 2:1–11). The water represents our humanity and our very real, but human, love. The wine represents the everlasting joy of divine love. At that wedding in Cana, the one who noticed that the wine had run dry was Mary, the mother of Jesus, and she turned to her son for help. Perhaps she knew the almost irresistible attraction of human love upon the divine heart. Of course, her son answered her plea. When the miracle was accomplished, the married couple had six stone jars filled to the brim with gallons of the finest wine, much better than they had before. When Jesus shares his love, he shares it superabundantly.

Mary's motherly concern, which she showed at the wedding at Cana, is mirrored in the actions of the Catholic Church. In the Sacrament of Matrimony, the Church, as did Mary at Cana, asks Jesus to change the water of human love into the wine of divine love. And to prepare couples for a long-lasting and happy marriage, the Church offers pre-Cana classes based on the wisdom it has developed over the past two thousand years. It's impossible to find a more experienced teacher. As divorce has grown ever more common, the Church has recognized that marriage preparation and support represent an "urgent need."[1]

St. John Paul II made love and marriage a priority of his priesthood and pontificate. He authored the groundbreaking book *Love and Responsibility* and delivered the talks later known as the theology of the body, both of which explored the importance of marriage and sexuality in revealing God's love to the world. His many encyclicals and speeches on the family are filled with practical insight into the problems that married couples face today.

At the urging of St. John Paul, the Pontifical Council for the Family identified a number of crucial lessons that would benefit couples the most,[2] including the following:

- Becoming united to one another in body, mind, and soul
- Learning to love your in-laws
- Bringing meaning and balance to your work life
- Taking stewardship of your finances
- Being a family at the service of other families
- Welcoming children with joy
- Accepting special-needs children with open arms
- Raising children to be successful saints
- Staying together through praying together
- Imitating the example of the Holy Family

Unlike most marriage-preparation courses and marriage-advice books, *The Four Keys to Everlasting Love* unpacks Church teaching on every recommended topic. Filled with explanations based on scripture, the *Catechism of the Catholic Church*, and the writings of St. John Paul II, the book also includes helpful advice for living the faith when confronted with modern-day challenges. It highlights real-world problems and solutions by sharing stories based on our work as pre-Cana teachers as well as detailed case studies, mostly drawn from patients seeking help in therapy. The case studies provide examples of the best and worst ways for couples to handle common pitfalls. Reflection questions encourage you to analyze how well the couple reacted and to think through what you might have done in their place.

The book also offers a glimpse inside our personal lives in the hopes that our experiences and struggles can help you in your journey. In these personal stories, the two of us did, said, and thought different things, so we can't always use the word "we." In most cases, we use "Manny" to refer to Dr. Santos and "I" to refer to Karee. But you also get to hear directly from Manny, in his own voice, in stories interspersed throughout the book.

How to Use This Book

The book is accessible enough for individuals or couples to read on their own, and informative enough to work as a text for a class. It speaks equally to engaged couples and married couples, since many of the issues they face are ultimately the same.

Although you can read this book on your own, we encourage you to read it together as a couple or in a small-group setting with other couples. Marriage is not something that can easily succeed on its own. Our marriages are nurtured by the example and friendship of other faith-filled couples. It helps to have companions on the journey. You might choose to use this book in a book club or parenting support group, as part of a parish marriage-enrichment program or pre-Cana program, or as part of your training to facilitate one of these groups.

We have included several features that you can adapt to meet your needs (or the needs of your group). Questions to jump-start conversation, action steps, and related *Catechism* quotes may be found at the end of each chapter. Appendix A offers tips on starting and running your own small discussion group, while appendix B provides a list of resources to help you explore a particular topic in greater depth. Free downloadable worksheets are also available on our website *Can We Cana?* (http://canwecana.blogspot.com).

Whether you're newly engaged or long married, we congratulate you on embarking on the experience of a lifetime. Consider this book to be like our wedding (or anniversary) gift to you: a gift of the four keys to loving faithfully, freely, fruitfully, and totally. May God's grace unlock the mysteries of spousal love, transform your hearts to be more like his, and bring you lifelong joy.

Yours in Christ,
Karee and Manny Santos

List of Abbreviations

CCC   *Catechism of the Catholic Church.* 2nd ed. Vatican City: Libreria Editrice Vaticana, 1997.

DCE   *Deus Caritas Est.* Benedict XVI's Encyclical Letter on Christian Love. Boston: Pauline, 2005.

DIM   *Divini Illius Magistri.* Pius XI's 1929 Encyclical Letter on the Christian Education of Youth. Kansas City, MO: Angelus Press, 2005.

EV   *Evangelium Vitae.* John Paul II's Encyclical Letter on the Gospel of Life. Boston: Pauline, 1995.

FC   *Familiaris Consortio.* John Paul II's Apostolic Exhortation on the Christian Family. Boston: Pauline, 1981.

HV   *Humanae Vitae.* Paul VI's Encyclical Letter on Human Life. Boston: Pauline, 1968.

LE   *Laborem Exercens.* John Paul II's Encyclical Letter on Human Work. Boston: Pauline, 1981.

LF   *Letter to Families (Gratissimam Sane).* John Paul II's Letter in the Year of the Family. Boston: Pauline, 1994.

LR   *Love and Responsibility.* By Karol Wojtyla (John Paul II). Boston: Pauline, 2013.

LS   *Lives . . . of the Saints for Every Day of the Year.* Hugo Hoever. Totowa, NJ: Catholic Book Publishing, 1999.

PP   *Prayer Primer: Igniting a Fire Within.* Thomas Dubay. Cincinnati: St. Anthony Messenger Press, 2002.

RC   *Redemptoris Custos (Guardian of the Redeemer).* John Paul II's Apostolic Exhortation on the Person and Mission of St. Joseph in the Life of Christ and of the Church. Boston: Pauline, 2014.

RM   *Redemptoris Mater (Mother of the Redeemer).* John Paul II's Encyclical on the Blessed Virgin Mary in the Life of the Pilgrim Church. Boston: Pauline, 2012.

TW   *The Way.* By Josemaría Escrivá de Balaguer. New York: Scepter, 2010.

PART I

CALLED TO BE FAITHFUL AND FORGIVING

Two Become One for Life

In each part of this book, we'll tell you about one of the four keys to everlasting love—the faithful, free, fruitful, and total love that Jesus gives to us and that we can share with our beloved. Part 1 of this book describes the call to faithfulness, which must be paired with the call to forgiveness.

People in love have an intense desire always to be true to each other in thought, word, and deed. The *Catechism of the Catholic Church* says they yearn for an "unbreakable union" (*CCC*, 1646), and they never want their differences to drive them apart (*CCC*, 2365).

And yet, all too often, reality intrudes. Husbands and wives *are* different from one another, and overcoming their differences can be a real struggle. Remaining faithful

1

to their lifelong promise requires constant, small, and loving acts of forgiveness.

The graces of the Sacrament of Matrimony and especially the Sacrament of Penance, or Confession, will help you to stay true to your marital vocation. Infidelity can present a powerful temptation. Christ would never betray his Church, but spouses sometimes do betray one another through adultery or abandonment (*CCC*, 2381, 2384–2386). God's grace in your marriage is a powerful force to keep potential infidelities at bay and usher you all the way to the doors of his heavenly kingdom.

Faithfulness to your spouse expands to encompass his or her family as well. When marriage joins two people, it also binds their two families together. Communication, compromise, and forgiveness are essential to cementing this bond. And the bonds you forge between your families can be the start of unity and peace in your corner of the world.

Turning Two into One

HOW TO OVERCOME THE DIFFERENCES THAT DIVIDE YOU

> So they are no longer two, but one flesh.
> —Matthew 19:6

When the two of us first met, about the only thing we had in common was our conviction that marriage should last "till death us do part." Manny was a first-generation Spanish American, longtime New Yorker, Catholic, Republican, extrovert, and optimist. In contrast, I could trace my family's roots at least to the American Revolution. I was proud to be a Virginian born and bred Episcopalian, Southern Democrat, and introvert with a slight tendency toward gloom.

We met briefly through a mutual friend, exchanging rushed greetings while crossing a busy street in midtown Manhattan, and the moment passed. "Who is she?" Manny asked his friend. "She's not your type," the friend immediately responded. Two years later, we met again. Despite our dissimilarities, Manny pursued me and won me. On our wedding day he escorted me out of the church to the sound of choir, trumpet, and organ blasting the "Hallelujah Chorus." Sixteen years and six kids later, we're still passionate about each other, marriage, and Jesus, although we've been stretched to our breaking point more than once.

To accommodate our differences as individuals, we've had to change, stretch, and be made new. "No one puts new wine into old wineskins; otherwise the new wine will burst the skins and will be spilled, and the skins will be destroyed," explained Jesus. "New wine must be put into fresh wineskins," he said (Lk 5:37–38). Our marriage is like that new wine, filled with astonishing grace, and we are like those old wineskins in danger of bursting if we can't accept our radical new life. So the two of us have not clung to our differences. Instead we have let in God to transform us.

Our marriage has had its good years and its not-so-good years. Most marriages will experience the truth of the first line of *A Tale of Two Cities*: "It was the best of times, it was the worst of times." No compelling story ever began with, "It was a routine time in which nothing ever changed and nothing unexpected ever happened." A tale with no ups and downs would be unworthy of a great adventure, and marriage is without a doubt an amazing adventure.

We have learned that only God can turn two into one because God's love is the glue that holds marriage together. God's strength has sustained us as we've negotiated personality, cultural, and religious differences. With his help, we have weathered intense health crises that exacted a heavy toll on us physically, emotionally, and spiritually. God is offering his strength to sustain you in your marriage, too.

Introvert Meets Extrovert: Appreciating Your Personality Differences

On our first date, we joined ten of Manny's colleagues at a barbecue restaurant. On the second date, a picnic and a concert at Central Park, he brought his best friend along, too. We didn't go out alone together until the third date. Manny jokes that he was afraid of me, but I think he just subscribes to the policy of the more, the merrier. He's the classic extrovert, and I'm the classic introvert.

Over the years, our personality differences have worked themselves out. The long and exhausting hours of a medical practice leave Manny little time or energy for big parties other than family events. Our six children are like a portable party anyway. Fun! Mess! Noise! Excitement! Introversion doesn't stand much of a chance in our house.

There's no point in us arguing over whether introversion or extroversion is a better way of life. Like hanging the toilet paper over or under the roll, there is no right answer. (Once you have kids, they'll throw your toilet paper all over the bathroom anyway.) Life has a way of busting us out of our self-imposed categories and certainties.

Our personalities are not set in stone. We are fundamentally free to become better people, more in tune with those around us, and more likely to act out of love rather than habit and basic inclination. An extroverted husband can help his wife relax and have fun, and an introverted wife can show her husband the spiritual riches of stillness. Striving to become one with our other half brings us closer to wholeness, even if we never completely iron out our differences.

Whether people are different doesn't determine how long their love will last. Although irreconcilable differences are frequently cited as the grounds for divorce, the vast majority of happy and unhappy couples have differences they will never reconcile, according to psychologist Dr. John Gottman.[1] Yielding in matters of personal preference can smooth over small problems. But fundamental disagreements usually require more intensive work.

Southern WASP Meets Spanish Catholic: Finding Common Cultural and Religious Ground

My parents (now known to our children as Oma and Opa) raised my brother and me as Episcopalians. The whole family faithfully attended church services every Sunday at R. E. Lee Memorial Episcopal Church. Although Opa's father was a Methodist minister and Oma was raised Baptist, Oma and Opa preferred the solemnity of the Episcopalian liturgy.

Manny's parents, Mama Carmen and José, emigrated from Spain to America in the 1960s. They came from southern Spain, an area near Seville where the pageantry and passion of Catholicism still hold sway. Both deeply devout, Mama Carmen and José taught their four children to treasure their faith.

Despite my career as a Manhattan litigator, I made time to sing every Sunday with the choir of St. Bartholomew's Episcopal Church on Park Avenue. Manny went to Mass every Sunday. When we dated, we did both—and as we became tired of going to two similar services, with the same readings proclaimed at both, it soon became a game of ecclesiastical chicken. Who would budge first?

In the end, since Manny's faith was more important to him than mine was to me, I joined Manny at Mass on Sundays, and we both started singing in a Catholic choir. After Mass, we visited Mama Carmen and José in Long Island, where Mama Carmen began teaching me the language and cuisine of her beloved home country while José discussed an unending array of philosophers and theologians. Manny's parents reminded me of my own globe-trotting mother and professorial father. Despite our different cultural backgrounds, Manny's parents made me feel right at home.

With our friends from choir, Manny and I started attending all-night adoration of the Blessed Sacrament every first Friday. As I watched frail-looking elderly ladies in black lace veils genuflect slowly and painfully on both knees every time they entered or exited a pew, the power of the Real Presence of Christ in the Eucharist was undeniable. The seeds for my conversion were sown, and I ultimately entered the Catholic Church in 1999 on the same day as our engagement party.

Unfortunately, not every couple is able to resolve their religious differences this neatly, or as quickly. Just as religion divides people all over the globe, spouses in interfaith marriages risk bringing that disunity into the heart of their own home, and that risk often intensifies with the arrival of children (*CCC*, 1634). As children reach the age for religious milestones such as Baptism, ceremonial circumcision, Confirmation, or bar or bat mitzvah, the parents are forced to face differences that may have been downplayed or ignored. All too often, one spouse may feel pressured to renounce previously cherished beliefs just to restore the peace—a short-term solution that can foster long-term resentment and regret.

To prevent these kinds of relational landmines, Catholics who wish to be married in the Church are reminded of their obligation to raise their children Catholic and must communicate this intention to their future spouse prior to the marriage (*CCC*, 1635). This comes as a surprise to some non-Catholics.

In our pre-Cana class, we counseled a Protestant groom-to-be who was complaining about all the restrictions and rules that were required to get married in the Catholic Church. "We're only doing it because my fiancée's grandmother wants us to," he grumbled. We told him that God was calling him to get married in the Catholic Church for some reason, even if the call came through his fiancée's grandmother. We encouraged him to treasure his future wife's Catholicism and focus on how they were both baptized Christians, seeking to follow God's will.

Emphasizing common ground is usually the best way to make an interreligious relationship work (*CCC*, 1634). Christians, Jews, and Muslims all worship the same God the Creator (*CCC*, 839–841). All Christians acknowledge Jesus as the Son of God and our Savior. Islam sees Jesus as a prophet. Many atheists and agnostics share a belief in basic human goodness and the duty to help one another. Focus more on what unites you than what divides you.

As long as they aren't confused, children can benefit from learning about more than one faith tradition. Parents may not feel it's appropriate to expose children to different types of religious ceremonies in different places of worship, but many families joyfully celebrate more than one type of religious holiday at home.

After years or decades of experiencing acceptance and sincere married love with a Catholic spouse, some non-Catholics may choose freely to convert (*CCC*, 1637). A friend of ours became a passionate Catholic convert from Judaism after being married ten years to her Catholic husband, who never pushed the issue of conversion. If you and your beloved have religious differences, pray that you both learn to love God more each day, and trust God to work in his own time and in his own way.

Pro-Lifer Meets Pro-Choicer: Disagreements as Opportunities for Growth

When Manny and I began dating, our private encounters often resembled a one-on-one debate club. Basking in the lovely summer weather, we would visit major Central Park landmarks and discuss hot-button issues on which we vehemently disagreed. While rowing on the lake we debated masturbation. Admiring the view from Belvedere Castle we argued about homosexuality. Lounging on the Great Lawn we clashed over abortion.

Fed up, I finally shouted, "Why don't you just go find a good Catholic girl?" Manny replied, "It's not that easy." Although Manny accepts all the doctrines of the Catholic Church, I soon learned how uncommon that was among Catholics. While the *Catechism of the Catholic Church* clearly opposes masturbation, homosexual acts, and abortion, almost half of all US Catholics disagree with the *Catechism* on these points (CCC, 2271, 2352, 2357). For example, according to some polls, 46 percent of Catholics say abortion should be legal and 43 percent believe that homosexual sex is morally acceptable.[2]

Even if you and your mate are both Catholic that doesn't mean you'll always be on the same page about Church teaching. And while it's a personal choice where you draw the line in the sand while you're dating, it's good to find out where you differ before you get married, preferably early on in the relationship. Then you have the chance to explore together what the Church really teaches and the reasons for it. Greater knowledge may help you settle disagreements.

We encountered our first serious conflict around the issue of abortion. Manny always fervently defended the Church's opposition to abortion based on the *Catechism*, which asserts that "human life must be respected and protected from the moment of conception" (*CCC*, 2270). Manny argued that a human zygote, a human embryo, and a human fetus are all human. In the womb or out, a human life is precious.

At that time, my views on abortion fell into what the pro-choice feminist Naomi Wolf once described as the "mushy middle." I knew I never wanted an abortion but thought other people should be free to make a different choice. And yet, as I listened to the impassioned arguments of my ardently pro-life suitor, my mind gradually began to change, and I was reminded of something my grandfather said. For my Methodist minister grandfather, the miraculous birth of Jesus from his virgin mother Mary was a reminder that every birth is miraculous. And in the story of the Annunciation, when the angel Gabriel seeks Mary's consent to bear the son of God in her womb, we celebrate not only the miracle of Jesus' birth but also the miracle of his *conception*. My eyes were opened to why the Church so staunchly defends life from its earliest stages.

In addition to these theological and philosophical arguments, Manny's clinical experience could not be easily disputed. He had seen firsthand how much abortion hurts the mothers and fathers left behind. Some of Manny's female patients experienced severe abortion-related depression decades after going through the procedure. I had also witnessed this on a more limited scale: I will never forget the day a male college acquaintance of mine broke down in tears as he explained that his ex-girlfriend had killed their child.

Fortunately, Manny and I were able to talk through most of our differences before we approached the altar.

Our "one-on-one debate club," founded on rules of loving and respectful dialogue, became a terrific basis for hashing out inevitable disagreements later in marriage, too. We learned to fight fair and to forgive, which built a strong foundation for our future relationship.

Health Meets Sickness:
Standing by Each Other in Troubled Times

Even the strongest foundation can be rocked by crises. Especially in times of difficulty, human love needs to find its roots in the divine. In the words of St. John Paul II, "Could we even imagine human love without the bridegroom [Christ] and the love with which he first loved to the end? Only if husbands and wives share in that love and in that 'great mystery' can they love 'to the end.' Unless they share in it, they do not know 'to the end' what love truly is and how radical are its demands. And this is undoubtedly very dangerous for them" (*LF*, 19).

For the two of us, the possibility of loving "to the end" came sooner than we ever dreamed it would. In December 2000, nine months after we got married and five months after we conceived our first child, Manny was diagnosed with a massive brain tumor. The neurosurgeon said the tumor needed to come out immediately.

When husbands and wives vow to love one another "in sickness and health," they don't expect serious medical issues to arise until age eighty or ninety. But of course sickness can hit at any time. In our circle of close friends and relatives, we've known several people in their thirties or forties diagnosed with serious illnesses. Twenty-eight-year-old Thomas Peters of the American Papist blog made headlines in 2013 when he became paralyzed from the chest down due to a diving accident only three months after getting married. Some marriages survive these crises and some don't. Are you committed to forever no matter what? Is your fiancé or spouse?

During the entire ordeal of that first brain surgery, we both prayed fervently and asked practically everyone we knew to pray for us. After Manny's amazingly quick initial recovery, one of our especially prayerful friends from church choir dubbed Manny the choir's "first miracle."

Manny's Story: Facing the Diagnosis

The "Sen Commandments" is what my wife and I dubbed the list of dos and don'ts from my neurosurgeon, Dr. Chandranath Sen. My brain tumor was about the size of a large orange, but the pathology report confirmed the tumor was benign and Dr. Sen assured us the surgery had been a success. "It popped right out," the doctor had said. "Get plenty of rest, make sure to eat, and no heavy lifting or straining."

Karee and I had only been married nine months, and at five months' pregnant her hormones were working overtime to keep me mesmerized by her beauty, prompting me to ask a delicate question: "Dr. Sen," I queried, "what about . . . physical intimacy?"

His answer was swift and decisive: "No. No sex for now." Like all the commandments, this one was difficult to adhere to at times, yet I knew the prohibition was for my benefit. Sex increases intracranial pressure, and this was not a good thing during the postoperative period.

Karee had been a pillar of strength for me throughout the diagnosis, the surgery, and the postsurgical period. No doubt she wondered what she would do if her husband died (leaving her widowed and with child), yet she had been steadfast, even stoic. My mother commented to me privately how impressed she was by Karee's strength. "She's a good woman, a strong woman," my mother said. I agreed.

Five years later, when the tumor returned (this time, the size of a cherry), the most difficult part of it all for me was telling my wife and my mother. I couldn't bear to see the pain and the fear on their faces.

This time around, I immediately sensed that Karee's reaction was different. I sensed her withdrawing emotionally and asking more questions about insurance coverage than usual. In private, I felt a strange sense of isolation, as though the Sen Commandments had been unofficially reinstated. As gently as I could, I asked her if she felt she was distancing herself unconsciously in order to protect herself. After a brief pause, she agreed that she was indeed reacting defensively to the news of my tumor. After that, the Sen Commandments were lifted, and my wife once again became the strong woman who had stood by me at the altar, prayed for me during my surgery, and nursed me back to health.

The first two tumors were only the beginning. Over time, Manny developed a total of four brain tumors, each one treated successfully. And yet the story never seemed to end. When Manny was diagnosed with his most recent brain tumor in 2012, I was struck by a horrible kind of grief, which I tried to hide from my husband. Instead of thinking that surely this brain tumor would be the last, I fell prey to the idea that tumor after tumor would grow until finally one would kill him.

What made matters worse, on some level, was the brain surgeon's refusal to operate. There had been so much scarring from previous surgeries and the tumor was so small and slow-growing that surgery posed almost as much risk as leaving it there. Although it was a relief to hear that surgery wasn't necessary, the presence of the tumor was a constant source of anxiety for me. It was harder to rely on each other, and it was harder to pray. Our faithfulness was being put to the test.

Manny's Story: The Tumor's Return

The fourth time around, Dr. Sen assured Karee and I that the tumor was small, less than one centimeter in diameter, and did not need to come out just yet. "No need for surgery" was music to my ears. "Careful observation," he called it. Every six to twelve months I would return for an MRI.

This time, my thoughts were not on me but on my father, also a psychiatrist with a thriving private practice, who had been diagnosed with a pituitary adenoma (the same tumor I had recovered from back in 2008). I also found myself increasingly overwhelmed by the pressures of maintaining my own full-time job while simultaneously covering my father's busy private practice.

Although Karee had initially taken the return of my tumor with remarkable grace, once again I sensed a distancing between us, and I found myself feeling alone and somewhat abandoned. My wife had gone into "battle mode," focused entirely on caring for our six young children. The prospect of losing me or, worse, of having to care for me as an invalid somewhere down the road had caused her to withdraw.

I continued working and fulfilling my obligations as a provider, but I found solace in exercise and alcohol. I sought escape from my bitter reality by exercising like a madman and then numbing myself with an inordinate indulgence in the fruit of the vine. Thankfully, I maintained regular contact with my spiritual director, meeting with him on average twice a month for guidance and confession. Fr. John was well aware of my situation, knew my family, and helped guide me through a very dark period in my life. I am certain that his prayers, along with those of my parents, my children, and my beloved wife, helped guide me from the depths of despair.

For now my "little friend" remains, nestled atop my right frontal lobe, gently reminding me of my mortality and exhorting me daily to thank God for the blessing of each new day.

Suffering Meets Hope:
Overcoming Fear through Faith

Although Manny had his deep-rooted faith and natural optimism to rely on, I was swamped with fear. I obsessed about the future, worrying that as a woman in her mid-forties with more than ten years out of the work force I would never be able to support six children and a sick husband on my own. I had no idea what to do.

We were deluged by well-meaning advice. One spiritual director warned that I was caught in a bizarre addiction to fear. "You retreat to fear like it's your safe place," she observed. "It's not really safe. And it's definitely not helping you." She counseled me to take one day at a time without revisiting the past or worrying about the future. "God wants us to live in the moment," she said, "because we can only sanctify the present moment. We can't change the past or control the future. The chance to do good or bad resides in the right here, right now."

Our friend Bette advised me to stay strong for my husband. "You have to be his rock," she told me. But I didn't want to be his rock. Manny had always been my stability, remaining peaceful in the face of my anxiety and staying calm and good humored in the face of my anger. The psalm we chose for our wedding proclaimed that God alone is "my rock and my salvation" (62:2). But secretly, I depended on my husband—not God—to be my rock.

Mama Carmen urged us to pray, as she did, that the tumor would simply disappear. Somehow I couldn't. I was tired of praying. I was tired of asking why, why us, why should this suffering come again. My resilience had floundered; whatever optimism I possessed had burned out. I was faced with the choice of either turning away from God or looking toward him still and saying, "Thy will be done." With the steadfast and faithful support of loved ones who kept praying even when I couldn't, I persevered. Eventually, suffering turned the corner into hope.

No one gets married expecting to suffer. And yet everyone does. Suffering is as inevitable as the rain, the winter, and the aches and twinges that come to our bodies as we age. Your marriage is your chosen battlefield in the war between good and evil that every soul must fight in order to attain heaven. People who leave their marriage only exchange one battlefield for another. It's impossible to avoid the battle itself.

Most people get married expecting to be happy. But happiness is not the absence of suffering. Happiness is staring suffering in the face and refusing to give it power over you, struggling to accept it while battling not to give in to despair. Happiness is trusting that if God is for us then no one and nothing can conquer us. Happiness is knowing that although life and love are not always easy, they are always worth it.

Much more than mere happiness, joy is a virtue, a habit of living that must be carefully cultivated. And true joy has its roots in the shape of a cross.[3] Joy is the decision to see the good in every person, challenge, or even tragedy that touches your life. Joy is the victory of hope, knowing that the good will not be lost. The joy that comes from Christ cannot be conquered, and it will never fade or dim.

Marriage will bring you roses, joy, and laughter. But at times you may also feel your back bowing under the weight of a cross you never thought would be yours to bear. Embrace the joy and thank God for it. Embrace the cross and ask Jesus for the strength to bear it. He will help you stay true to one another in good times and bad. He will aid you in appreciating each other's strengths and forgiving one another's weaknesses. And he will give you the sacraments of his Church to sustain you along your way.

Bonus Material
Conversation Starters

- What personality, cultural, or religious differences do the two of you have? How have you handled them so far?
- How often do you discuss important and difficult topics? How often do you apologize if what you say hurts or angers the other person?
- Think of the biggest crisis that has hit your relationship. What character strengths or weaknesses were revealed in each of you?
- Which friends and family members can you rely on to support your marriage?

Action Plan

Plan a date to remind you of when you first met. Go to the same place or do the same activity. Talk over how much has changed, and thank God for bringing you together!

Catechism Corner

"Man and woman were made 'for each other'—not that God left them half-made and incomplete: he created them to be a communion of persons, in which each can be 'help-mate' to the other" (CCC, 372).

2.

Turning Good Marriages into Pathways to Glory

IT'S A SACRAMENT; IT'S A VOCATION; IT'S A ROAD MAP TO HEAVEN!

Sacramental marriage "aims at a deeply personal unity, the unity that, beyond union in one flesh, leads to forming one heart and soul."
—Pope John Paul II, *Familiaris Consortio*, 13

Marriage can be good. With effort, it can be very good. But it takes God to make the union glorious—a foretaste of heaven, in a sense. God can help you find the glory in lifelong commitment through all the highs and lows. God calls you together, he binds you together in a mystical way through the Sacrament of Matrimony, and he sets you on the path to heaven. He wants husbands and wives to seek each other's salvation and redemption by offering all they have without holding anything back.

Sacramental Channels of Grace

The first step in cooperating with God's beautiful plan for our married lives is to realize that "God himself is the author of marriage" (*CCC*, 1603). In the beginning of human history, God created us for love. Genesis, the first book of the Bible, reveals the wonderful mystery of our humanity as male and female, designed to become one flesh in the marriage covenant. "Holy Scripture affirms that man and woman were created for one another: 'It is not good that the man should be alone.' The woman, 'flesh of his flesh,' his equal, his nearest in all things, is given to him by God as a 'helpmate'; she thus represents God from whom comes our help. 'Therefore a man leaves his father and his mother and cleaves to his wife, and they become one flesh'" (*CCC*, 1605 quoting Gn 2:18–25).

When Jesus came to earth, he raised marriage to the dignity of a sacrament, a visible outer sign of an inner grace. In teaching about God's plan for marriage, Jesus repeated the message of Genesis, insisting that a married couple is "no longer two, but one flesh." In a stunningly definitive pronouncement, Jesus declared, "What God has joined together, let no one separate" (Mt 19:6).

Sacramental marriage is more than an agreement that two people will stay together "as long as it works out." As the *Catechism* states, "By its very nature the gift of the person must be lasting and irrevocable," because "love seeks to be definitive; it cannot be an arrangement 'until further notice'" (*CCC*, 1646).

The graces of sacramental marriage extend far beyond the bride and groom to the whole community. This lesson came home to us in a rather surprising way on our wedding day. In planning our wedding ceremony, we asked the celebrant to give Holy Communion only to us, so that my Protestant family would not feel left out.

But in the middle of the wedding, to our shock and cha-
grin, the pastor announced that the Eucharist would be
offered to all Catholics in a state of grace—and added that
non-Catholics could receive a blessing. So people on both
sides of the church stood up and approached the altar.

Although we were initially upset at the pastor's
impromptu announcement, we realized later that the ceremony happened exactly as it should have. The center of
our wedding Mass was not us and it was not our families.
The center of our wedding Mass, like the center of every
Mass, was Christ in the Eucharist.

To say that marriage is a sacrament also means that as
a married couple you receive special graces from God. As
John Paul II stated, "The Spirit which the Lord pours forth
gives a new heart, and renders man and woman capable
of loving one another as Christ has loved us" (*Familiaris
Consortio* [*FC*], 13).

This grace of the Holy Spirit, given through the Sacrament of Matrimony, is what makes impossible things
possible. It is this grace that will fill you with the strength
"to forgive one another, to bear one another's burdens,
to 'be subject to one another out of reverence for Christ,'
and to love one another with supernatural, tender, and
fruitful love" (*CCC*, 1642 quoting Eph 5:21).

Seek Help from the Sacraments

These graces of matrimony build in a very real way upon
the graces of Baptism and Confirmation (*CCC*, 1533). Baptism is "the door which gives access to the other sacraments," meaning that a person must first be baptized in
order to receive any of the other sacraments (*CCC*, 1213).
Confirmation completes baptismal grace and enriches us
"with a special strength of the Holy Spirit" (*CCC*, 1285).

These sacraments support us in our special mission as married couples—a mission of service to others (*CCC*, 1533–1534).

Although we can receive Baptism and Confirmation only once, there are other sacraments we can return to again and again for help. These are the Sacraments of the Anointing of the Sick, Penance and Reconciliation, and the Eucharist.

Manny and I have a special fondness for the Sacrament of the Anointing of the Sick, which is available not just to the dying but also to anyone with a life-threatening illness or surgery (*CCC*, 1514–1515). Manny received the Anointing of the Sick before each of his brain surgeries. This sacrament is meant to bring healing of both the soul and the body, if God wills, renewing the sick person's faith and removing "the temptation to discouragement and anguish in the face of death" (*CCC*, 1520). As we well know, the temptation to discouragement and despair is all too real.

While the Anointing of the Sick is one sacrament of healing, the Sacrament of Penance and Reconciliation, commonly called confession, is another. Although the Church obligates us to go only once a year, confession is available as often as needed (*CCC*, 1457–1458). Many people we know go to confession monthly or even weekly if they're determined to grow closer to God and progress in their spiritual life.

We've found sacramental confession to be absolutely crucial in a marriage. It heals us from sin and helps us to grow in holiness (*CCC*, 1421, 1426). The grace we receive through this sacrament also helps us to fight temptations or overcome bad habits that are destructive to our marriages. And the more often we confess our sins, the firmer our resolve grows to do right and turn away from wrong.

Sin obstructs the channels through which the sacramental graces of matrimony flow. It clouds our vision and interferes with our ability to hear God's call. Even something as common as deliberately skipping Sunday Mass can put a stain of sin on our soul. Many people don't realize that the Church considers skipping Sunday Mass to be a grave (or mortal) sin (*CCC*, 2181). We astonished our friend Tom when we told him, and he grumbled that he'd committed a lot worse sins in his life. But after he went to confession for it, Tom texted us: "Thanks. Best confession I ever had."

Confession returns us to a state of grace and allows us to receive Holy Communion worthily (*CCC*, 1457). "Food cannot profit a body that is dead; neither can Holy Communion, the divine food of the soul, profit a soul that is dead to the grace of God."[1] Confession heals and enlivens your soul.

In Search of Everlasting Love

*Can Sacramental Confession Help a
Married Couple Heal Their Relationship?*

When Agnieszka got pregnant while she and Józéf were dating, the couple decided to marry quickly and so skipped the church wedding. They intended to marry in the Church later but somehow never got around to it. For fifteen years Józéf worked in the bakery chain owned by Agnieszka's parents. Józéf complained to his wife that he did all the work for little money and even less respect, but Agnieszka refused to take Józéf's side against her parents.

Feeling angry and emasculated, Józéf began going to strip clubs. In one of the clubs he met a waitress who treated him like he was the only thing in her world, and he wound up having an affair with her. When Agnieszka found out, she demanded a separation even after her husband stopped the affair. Józéf felt helpless to save their marriage. He realized he could not fix the problem himself and needed intensive professional intervention.

Reflection Questions

1. How do you think Agnieszka's getting pregnant before the wedding affected their future marriage?
2. What do you think led to Józéf's infidelity?
3. How do you think confession might help Józéf?

Manny's Diagnosis

Because of Agnieszka's pregnancy the couple rushed into marriage, perhaps before they felt fully committed to it. This ambivalence played out in their saying they wanted to get married in the Church but never going through with it. Józéf's infidelity, while inexcusable, had its roots in the relationship's rocky start and in his wife's refusal to choose him over her family. He made things worse when he exposed himself to temptation by visiting a strip club.

Confession was a first step in healing, helping him to admit and accept responsibility for his destructive behavior and clearing a path for grace to operate. But confession needed to be accompanied by a strong commitment to change his behavior. In therapy, as part of his treatment plan, Józéf was advised to follow the "3R Rule":

> **R**econciliation (go to confession to make a fresh start as often as needed)
>
> **R**osary (pray it daily for his marriage and his family)

Ring (always wear his wedding band as a symbol
of his continued fidelity)

A year later, Agnieszlea and Jozéf were still separated,
but they had not divorced and were continuing to work on
their problems.

Even above and beyond sacramental confession, the most
powerful spiritual aid for your marriage comes from the
Sacrament of the Eucharist, which is "the source and summit of the Christian life" (*CCC*, 1324). It is a banquet that
nourishes the life of grace we received at Baptism (*CCC*,
1391–1392). It is a memorial of the love with which Jesus
loved us to the end (*CCC*, 1380), the love we are called
to share with our spouses. It is the "Sacrament of sacraments," providing fuel for our faith and sustenance for
our spirits (*CCC*, 1211). Jesus in the Eucharist waits for us
in Mass every day, just as he waits at the altar for couples
on their wedding day. Accept the love he offers!

One with Each Other, One with God

Throughout your years together the sacramental life of
the Church can strengthen and uphold you; there you
will experience the truth Christ promised, that "where
two or three or gathered in my name, I am there among
them" (Mt 18:20). In marriage, two people come together
in God's name and he is there with them.

Through God's sustaining presence in your marriage,
you become living witnesses of the awe-inspiring and
unbreakable bond between Christ and the Church (see
Eph 5:31–32). By remaining faithful in marriage, especially

when tested, spouses demonstrate Christ's fidelity to his people even when they turn away from him through sin.

Remember that your marriage is bigger than you, bigger than both of you, and a valid marriage cannot be dissolved even if your spouse is doing his or her level best to drive you round the bend (*CCC*, 1640). The *Catechism* explains, "It can seem difficult, even impossible, to bind oneself for life to another human being. This makes it all the more important to proclaim the Good News that God loves us with a definitive and irrevocable love, that married couples share in this love, that it supports and sustains them, and that by their own faithfulness they can be witnesses to God's faithful love" (*CCC*, 1648).

The Church recognizes that "there are some situations in which living together becomes practically impossible" (*CCC*, 1649). This is particularly true in the case of an abusive relationship. Separation, or even a civil divorce, may be necessary if it is the only way to protect all the family members (*CCC*, 2383). But in the eyes of the Church, a couple that obtains a civil divorce is still married (*CCC*, 2382). Neither person is free to remarry unless Church authorities determine through an annulment, or "decree of nullity," that the first marriage was invalid from the beginning.

An annulment is not the Catholic version of a civil divorce. Generally speaking, annulments are granted when couples did not or could not freely consent to the marriage, frequently because of psychological deficiencies. But whatever happens after the couple takes their vows does not affect the question of whether the marriage was valid. Annulments are also routinely granted when baptized Catholics marry outside the Church without permission from the bishop, since that kind of marriage is not considered to be either valid or sacramental. The full panoply of graces is available only to those in valid and sacramental marriages.

In Search of Everlasting Love

What Difference Does a Sacramental Marriage Make?

Ariana, a cradle Catholic, fell in love with Jason, a Jewish man. They got married in the Catholic Church by a priest and with all the proper dispensations. The marriage was valid but not sacramental, since sacramental marriages can exist only between two baptized people. After Ariana and Jason had their third child, their marriage fell apart despite Ariana's efforts to save it.

Ariana struggled both financially and personally after her divorce from Jason. When she met Nick, who wanted to marry her and be another father to her three children, Ariana was thrilled. But Ariana and Nick couldn't get married in the Catholic Church because Ariana had not obtained an annulment of her first marriage. Nick, a fallen-away Catholic, insisted that getting married in the Church wasn't that important. Despite her misgivings, Ariana agreed, and they were married by a justice of the peace.

Very shortly thereafter, Nick and Ariana's relationship was hit by several crises. Nick lost his job and fought constantly with Ariana's sons, who resented Nick's authoritarian style of discipline. The atmosphere in the house became so toxic that Nick had to move out. "The reason we had so many problems," Ariana realized, "is that we didn't have Jesus in our marriage."

Reflection Questions

1. What similarities do you see between Ariana's first and second marriage?

2. How might Ariana and Nick's relationship have been strengthened if they had waited for her to obtain an annulment?

3. What do you think put the most strain on Ariana and Nick's relationship?

Manny's Diagnosis

Although Ariana's faith mattered a lot to her, in both instances she chose husbands who did not share her faith. In her second marriage, she felt particularly pressured by her personal and financial crises and by Nick's insistence that marrying in the Church was unimportant.

The annulment process is meant to inspire self-examination and self-reflection—to shed light on the problems with the first marriage so the same problem doesn't occur again. If Ariana had waited for an annulment, she might have realized that Nick was not the right husband for her, or she might have asked that he treat her faith with more respect. With one less strain on the marriage and more grace to nourish it, it might have survived.

All validly married couples receive God's grace to help them love, forgive, and be faithful. But couples united in the Sacrament of Matrimony have been blessed with the grace to take natural love to a supernatural level. Treasured by Christ the Bridegroom as members of his Body, they are called and empowered to love to the highest degree, the degree that Christ loved us—to forgive seventy times seven times, to do the humblest chore out of love, and to die to self in order to live and love for others.

The demands of faithful marriage may seem humanly impossible at times. But we can live up to them with God's help. As Jesus says in scripture, for human beings it is impossible, "but not for God; for God all things are possible" (Mk 10:27).

God Has Called You Each by Name

God gives each of us a vocation, calling some to the priesthood, some to religious life, and some to marriage. This vocation is God's plan for you, "a specific mission to accomplish, a concrete task to fulfill." It is his loving design for you conceived from all eternity.[2]

The vocation of marriage is a radical call to serve others, beginning with our spouse, our children, and our God (*CCC*, 1533–1534). It is not a call to tame and self-indulgent comfort; rather, it is a call to struggle, adventure, sacrifice, and glory. The *Catechism* describes the beauty and the joy of embracing this vocation as joining in a magnificent "bond between two believers, now one in hope, one in desire, one in discipline, one in the same service!"[3] By answering the call to serve others through our marriage, we become living contradictions of the devil and his battle cry, "I will not serve" (*The Way* [*TW*], 413).

Marriage is a common but highly important vocation in the eyes of the Church. As John Paul II encouraged us, "To those of you whom Christ is calling to the vocation of married life I say this: be assured of the Church's love for you. Christian family life and lifelong fidelity in marriage are so needed in the world today."[4]

God doesn't necessarily send special signs that you have found "the one" person to marry. As most of our friends told us when we were considering marriage, the signs are in your heart—"you just know." This knowledge of whether to marry, whom to marry, and when to marry comes from deep thought, introspection, prayer, and a willingness to listen to God. It is a type of discernment, similar to discerning a priestly vocation. At the end of the discerning process, you will find a sign in your heart, a sign of peace and calm that inaudibly communicates God's pleasure with your decision. It may take time to recognize the signs, but that's perfectly okay.

The first book of Samuel in the Old Testament contains a wonderful story about how Samuel finally learned to listen to God's call. When Samuel was a boy, his mother gave him to be the servant of Eli the priest. Samuel was sleeping in the temple when he heard someone calling him. He got up and ran to Eli, who said, "I did not call; lie down again." Samuel went back to sleep, and again he heard somebody calling. Again he ran to Eli, who said once more, "I did not call." When Samuel heard the voice the third time, Eli recognized that the Lord was calling Samuel. So Eli told Samuel that if he heard the voice again he should answer, "Speak, Lord, for your servant is listening." The Lord did call Samuel again and revealed a great prophecy to him. Then "all Israel . . . knew that Samuel was a trustworthy prophet of the Lord" (3:3–20).

Even if you don't recognize God's call at first, he will not give up on you. He will keep calling. This story has a parallel in the lives of some friends of ours. Our friend Joe had to ask Sabrina out for a date several times (Joe says it's at least ten) before she finally said yes to him. Now they're married with seven beautiful children. They kept listening to and following God's call for their marriage. So keep asking God about his plans for your marriage, the specific mission you are to accomplish, and the concrete task you are to fulfill. Keep listening to his call, and he won't guide you astray.

Marriage Is a Path to Heaven, Not Heaven on Earth

St. Teresa of Avila famously quipped that our life on earth is like a bad night in a rough hotel. (At least in marriage we have a warm body to curl up next to.) But this path to heaven we call life is arduous. It brings equal parts joy and sadness, and someone to hold our hand through the hard times can make all the difference.

God wants us to be holy, to be sanctified, and to be happy with him forever in heaven. John Paul II stressed that for spouses, our vocation to marriage is how we achieve sanctification, or holiness, during our time on earth (*FC*, 56). So saying that marriage is a means of sanctification is like saying your marriage is your road map to heaven. That is different from saying your marriage will be heaven on earth!

Whether your marriage turns out to be easy and loving, or not so easy and not so loving, it is still the means of your sanctification. A difficult or annoying spouse can help you to holiness faster than one who is more amenable. So whenever Manny or I do something we realize is truly annoying, we remind each other, "Remember, dear, I'm the means of your sanctification!"

It's comforting to realize that God does not require greatness from our marriage. All he asks from us is littleness and love, and he will turn it into greatness and glory (see Mt 25:21). Caring attentiveness in little things is like a shortcut to the pearly gates. As St. Josemaría advised, "Do everything for love. In that way there will be no little things: everything will be big. Perseverance in the little things for love is heroism" (*TW*, 813).

Being faithful in little things simply means caring for one another and the children. Our Lord promised the kingdom of heaven to the caretakers, saying, "I was hungry and you gave me food, I was thirsty and you gave me something to drink . . . sick and you took care of me" (Mt 25:35–36). This is what husbands and wives do, day in and day out, when they work to bring home money for the family, when they prepare meals, and when they nurse each other and the children through illnesses. Every token of affection you give to your spouse is like a kiss on the face of God.

Married life isn't a sprint; it's a marathon. Keep striving each day, and you can make it to the finish line.

Seek Help from the Saints

If you've ever run a footrace, you've encountered people along the route who hand you cups of water to help you keep going. The saints are like those people, rooting for your success and the success of your marriage, encouraging you to drink the living water of Jesus in the sacraments.

Married saints in particular can be your best role models and your most devoted friends. Reach out to them and get to know them! Married saints run the gamut from those with wonderful marriages to those with terrible marriages. The Bible and Church tradition are filled with stories of saints with good marriages, such as Mary and Joseph, Anne and Joachim (parents of Mary and grandparents of Jesus), and Elizabeth and Zechariah (Mary's cousins and the parents of John the Baptist).

St. Gianna Beretta Molla is a more modern example of a holy woman with a good marriage. In her short but happy marriage of seven years, St. Gianna worked as a physician and gave birth to four children. Letters to and from her husband, Pietro, show a touching and devoted love between the couple. When Gianna encountered medical complications in her fourth pregnancy, she told her doctors to save the child first and then the mother. Her fourth child, a daughter, was delivered safely in 1962, but St. Gianna died one week later. Pietro raised their children to adulthood and lived to see his wife's canonization ceremony.

Some saints did not enjoy the love and devotion of their husbands. Saints with difficult marriages include St. Monica, whose incessant prayers converted both her pagan husband and her wayward son (who dabbled in many different religions and had a longtime mistress with whom he conceived a child). St. Monica's son turned out to be St. Augustine, the great theologian and Doctor of the Church.

Venerable Cornelia Connelly, who lived in the nineteenth century, also suffered greatly in her marriage. Cornelia was a Lutheran who became Episcopalian and then Catholic, following the lead of her husband, Pierce. When Pierce announced that he felt called to the Catholic priesthood, Cornelia agreed to take a vow of chastity. Soon thereafter, she founded a new religious order. Changing his mind once more, Pierce left the priesthood, returned to being Episcopalian, and sued Cornelia in court, demanding that she live with him again as his wife. She refused and ultimately won the lawsuit, but Pierce succeeded in alienating her children from her.

The example of Venerable Cornelia shows that human beings are always free to reject grace, to ignore God's call, and to give up striving for heaven. The consequences of turning away from God in this way can be disastrous for a marriage. But if both spouses do their utmost to cooperate with God's plan for them, the results can be glorious.

Bonus Material

Conversation Starters

- Why did you choose each other? How did you know you had found "the one"?
- Why did you decide in favor of (or against) getting married in the Catholic Church?
- How have you seen the graces of the sacrament at work in your lives and in your relationship?
- Who do you think has an exceptionally good marriage and why? Do you have a favorite married saint who would be a good role model?

Action Plan

Show affection every day. Hug your spouse when he or she leaves and comes home again. Go to confession when you hurt each other; go to Mass to say thanks for each other. Choose a married saint as your family's patron, and read a book or watch a movie about your chosen saint. And if you didn't get married in the Church, talk to your pastor about having your marriage convalidated—it would make a lovely anniversary celebration and a wonderful example to your children!

Catechism Corner

Husbands and wives should constantly try "to forgive one another, to bear one another's burdens, to 'be subject to one another out of reverence for Christ,' and to love one another with supernatural, tender, and fruitful love" (CCC, 1642 quoting Eph 5:21).

3.

Turning Union into Communion

EXTENDING YOUR LOVE TO
YOUR IN-LAWS AND BEYOND

All members of the family . . . have the grace and
responsibility of building, day by day, the communion of persons, making the family "a school
of deeper humanity."
—Pope John Paul II, *Familiaris Consortio*, 21

Weddings have a powerful ability to draw relatives closer
together, as we were delighted to discover on our own
wedding day. Back in 2000, my uncle had been estranged
from his parents and siblings for twenty years. At the
urging of his new wife, he had begun to make small
steps toward reconciliation with his family. Manny and
I invited him to our wedding, and to our amazement,
he and his wife accepted. My uncle saw his mother and
siblings there for the first time in decades and through

the healing graces of his own marriage found strength to mend the broken family ties.

It was fidelity to his wife's wishes that helped my uncle put past hurts and disagreements behind him. In return, his mother and siblings received him with all the love and forgiveness in their hearts. God willing, your strongly unified marriage can also join your extended families together in what Pope John Paul II called a "community of life and love" (*FC*, 17).

Leaving Your Family of Origin

After marriage, priorities rightly shift. Although you love your parents as much as ever, pleasing your spouse takes center stage. Marriage creates a new family and causes a natural separation from your family of origin. As the Bible beautifully expresses it, "Therefore a man leaves his father and his mother and clings to his wife, and they become one flesh" (Gn 2:24).

This transition can affect your parents more strongly than you might think. One mother recounted the story of her adult son rhapsodizing about his fiancée, "Mom, she's everything to me!" This made his mother silently question, "And what am I? Chopped liver?" It takes time for parents to get used to the shifting of priorities in their child's life. Sometimes a certain grief goes along with it. Oma struggled with the feeling that she lost each of her children for good on their wedding day. Manny kindly promised Oma that he would bring me home to her in Virginia more often.

While Oma worried about losing me, I worried about where Manny's loyalties would lie if it came down to a choice between Mama Carmen and me. Manny has always had a strong relationship with his mother, who has firm opinions and a powerful personality to back them up. He won my heart (again) over a particular incident during our engagement period when he deliberately and respectfully took my side against hers.

Manny had just graduated from medical residency, and the whole family attended the graduation ceremony together. But the following weekend, I already had long-standing plans to attend a singing workshop with some of my friends from as far away as Japan. Mama Carmen wanted me to stay for the post-graduation festivities and cancel my weekend away. Manny explained to her that this weekend mattered to me and that he supported my decision to go. This signaled to me that, in the years to come, he would continue to put our marriage first.

What does it mean to honor your parents after marriage? It means something very different from the obedience a child living at home must give his or her parents. When adult children move out and form their own families, they honor their parents by showing them respect (*CCC*, 2217). Along with the increased responsibilities of marriage comes an increased autonomy from parental control. Sometimes, in order to create a new family, it's necessary to draw firm boundaries to protect it. But creating a new family does not mean breaking all ties with the old one.

In Search of Everlasting Love

*How Do Wedding Conflicts Point to
Underlying Family Conflicts?*

Roberto and Ella, both Filipino Catholics, began dating and soon considered marriage. Ella's mother had been the dominant force in her family. Ella herself had very low self-esteem. Ella's mother approved strongly of Roberto but constantly warned Ella that she wasn't good enough for him.

When Roberto and Ella became engaged, Ella's mother wanted to handle the wedding preparations. What Ella needed, however, was to put some distance between herself and her mother. Roberto and Ella decided to hire a wedding planner so that wedding preparation would be handled through a neutral third party. The wedding planner stuck to a very strict budget, as the couple wanted, and Ella was able to keep her mother from taking control of the entire process.

Reflection Questions

1. What did the wedding planning process reveal about Ella's relationship with her mother?

2. Did any family members create conflict as you prepared for your wedding? How did you work together to resolve these conflicts?

3. In what ways can difficult family relationships color a marital relationship?

Manny's Diagnosis

Ella's mother tried to control the wedding planning just as she had always exerted control over Ella. Roberto protected Ella and their marriage when he found a way for them to set boundaries in a respectful and nonconfrontational way. Roberto and Ella will not always be able to avoid family conflict by turning things over to a neutral third party like the wedding planner, however. Ella will need Roberto's help to build her self-esteem and the courage to stand up to her mother on her own.

Although the new family you create will be your own, your parents still have valuable experience that can help you in establishing your new married life together. You do not have to follow their advice, but if you listen respectfully, you still might learn something. In addition, marriage and parenthood may help you gain new insight into your parents, because you're going through the same life experiences they've already gone through. Your commitment to your spouse can ultimately strengthen your commitment to your parents, and vice versa.

In most cases, what your parents and your spouse's parents really want is for their children to be happy in marriage and in life. Opa made a special effort to reach out to Manny in the days before our wedding. At our rehearsal dinner, Opa pulled Manny aside and told him, "You and I are the only ones who know how special she truly is." When Opa walked me down the aisle, and when we danced together at the wedding reception to the song "My Girl," I felt he treasured me and, at the same time, was willing to let me go. Isn't that what fatherly love is?

Communicating with Caring

Each family is different because each couple is different. And yet every Christian family is "a sign and image of the communion of the Father and the Son in the Holy Spirit" (*CCC*, 2205). We are called to love each other and every member of our extended families with a godly love.

The best way you can help your spouse integrate into your family of origin is to keep the marriage relationship strong. What makes a marriage strong, on a practical level, is learning how to make decisions together, solve problems together, and communicate in a way the other can understand. A strong marriage can better resist potential conflicts caused by in-laws and extended family members.

The basics of marital communication are simple. Set aside a quiet time and a peaceful atmosphere to talk regularly about things so they don't get a chance to build up or fester. If something bothers you, speak up. If you want something, state it clearly.

In the heat of an argument, emotions can sometimes swamp reason, and you need time and space to think things through on your own. If you are having trouble controlling your emotions, table the conversation until you've both calmed down. Consider writing down your thoughts in a letter or e-mail to help you sort them out. Finally, if hurtful words are exchanged, always forgive and ask forgiveness. As it says in scripture, don't let the sun go down on your anger (see Eph 4:26).

Communication won't always succeed in crafting the perfect compromise, however. In situations where the two of us can't come to an agreement, I like to think I let Manny win. He is the head of the family, after all, so I'd rather let him lead. But not *every* time! Manny points to my absolute refusal to get a dog for the kids despite their repeated entreaties. From my perspective, my refusal to add four-footed creatures to our family enables me to retain my sanity; it's really a matter of survival. Fortunately, we've been able to keep a sense of humor about it (so far). But the decision remains with him and me. No one else gets a vote—not our kids and certainly not our parents.

When you and your mate are having trouble seeing eye to eye, it's generally not helpful to ask your parents (or your spouse's parents) to pick sides in the dispute. One couple we know who did this wound up divorced six months after getting married. Especially if both spouses

just want to dig in their heels, this is a marital problem—
not a problem that needs to involve the whole family.
Talk, pray, revisit the issue, pray some more, but keep it
between the two of you (unless you find you need professional help).

Some decisions that directly affect extended family
members do require input from them—and the same
respectful communications principles apply. If you work
hard at building up these skills between the two of you,
when it comes time to negotiate a family-wide compromise like the fairest system of exchanging holiday and
birthday gifts, you will have a great basis for conflict
resolution.

Fortunately, conflict resolution skills can be learned
in many settings. When I worked for a Japanese corpo-
ration in Tokyo, I learned invaluable lessons in how to
broker a group-wide consensus. In the Japanese business
world, in order to finalize even a simple decision such as
choosing a restaurant for a business dinner, the person
guiding the decision must talk to each person involved,
again and again, until everyone reaches agreement. This
type of carefully negotiated consensus can add a lot to
family harmony.

Another useful technique is called active listening. In
active listening, you listen carefully and then repeat back
what you think you just heard to make sure you got it
right ("So, what you're saying is . . ."). By listening to the
other person in order to understand rather than to gather
ammunition to win the argument, you'll gain precious
insight into the people who matter to you regardless of
the outcome.

It's particularly important to examine your own pre-
conceptions. Do you hold a certain opinion because of
how you were raised? Your spouse's family may prefer a
different way that will work equally well or even better

if you're open to it. For example, I grew up in a small family where everyone exchanged gifts on Christmas. But Manny's family was so large that our Christmas gift list soon expanded to more than two dozen people. So after extended discussion, we agreed that adults would give presents to children but not to each other. Every few years we renegotiate, as more adults and children join our ever-growing ranks, and we struggle to do what's fair for everyone.

Conflicts and compromises with people we love actually draw us out of our own self-centeredness, orienting our lives and our actions as much around the other as around ourselves. This is a good thing. This is how strong marriages and families are built.

Embracing Your In-Laws

The Bible contains both flattering and unflattering portraits of relationships with in-laws. The Old Testament story of Ruth, for example, highlights Ruth's touching loyalty to her mother-in-law, Naomi. Ruth was a Moabite, and Naomi came from Bethlehem. After Naomi's husband and two sons died, Naomi planned to return to Bethlehem alone, letting her daughters-in-law return to their own families. But Ruth "clung to" Naomi and would not leave, saying, "Where you go, I will go; where you lodge, I will lodge; your people shall be my people, and your God my God" (Ru 1:14, 16).

The story of Jacob and his father-in-law, Laban, provides a stark contrast. After working for his father-in-law for twenty years, Jacob and his family took their household possessions and flocks and fled to another country without telling Laban. When Laban pursued Jacob and demanded to know why he had left, Jacob admonished the older man, who had continuously cheated Jacob of his fair wages (see Gn 31:40–41). Jacob finally concluded, "If the God of my father . . . had not been on my side, surely now you would have sent me away empty-handed" (Gn 31:42).

Most people's relationship with their in-laws falls somewhere in between Ruth's devotion and Jacob's determination to escape. But without question, integrating yourself into your spouse's family frequently proceeds along a very bumpy road. This integration begins in earnest during the engagement period, particularly as both sets of parents weigh in with their expectations about the wedding. As opinions and arguments fly, it helps to remember that the good qualities you cherish in your spouse-to-be were probably instilled by his or her parents.

Frankly, planning our wedding resembled peace negotiations in the aftermath of World War III. For example, Oma wanted no alcohol at the reception, and Manny's brother insisted on an open bar. We compromised with an open bar for the cocktail hour. Sobriety and frugality were tempered by hospitality.

Another clash of opinions arose over the floral arrangements. As part of the regular reception package, the hotel included a bud vase with a single red rose at each table. Mama Carmen thought we needed more, but I didn't want to pay for something that was already being provided. So Mama Carmen and José broke the deadlock by graciously agreeing to pay for exquisite table arrangements. Generosity and love of beauty won the day. And on and on, the negotiations continued. Every conflict taught us more about what the two families valued, and every compromise allowed us to combine the best of both.

Embracing the Extended Family

The commandment to honor, respect, and love our parents and our spouse's parents actually extends more broadly to all our relatives (*CCC*, 2199). The *Catechism* states, "In our brothers and sisters we see the children of our parents; in our cousins, the descendants of our ancestors" (CCC, 2212). One day your parents will be gone. Your brothers and sisters will be all that's left of your family of origin. Cherish them.

What does this mean, exactly, to cherish someone who doesn't live nearby? It can be different from one family to the next. Some brothers and sisters call each other a few times a year, and some call each other every day. Some send handwritten letters and home-baked cookies; others e-mail or send a gift card to the sibling who is going through a tough time. Some won't speak to each other at all. Different families have different degrees of closeness. What is more, your spouse's family may interact very differently from yours. It will take time to negotiate the relationship you have with your in-laws and to get a sense of what will be welcome and reciprocated. It's important to practice generosity and patience, and not to project your expectations onto them as the only "right" way to be a family.

I have one brother, Harrison, who is eight years younger than I am. Oma decided to raise us as "two only children" so she could devote herself completely to us, one at a time. I went away to school at age fourteen, when Harrison was only six. We love each other dearly, but we don't talk or e-mail often, and we live far enough away that we see each other only once or twice a year.

In contrast, Harrison and I both married spouses from large, close families. Harrison's wife frequently talks to and visits her parents and brothers. Manny's siblings all still live in the New York area. We even live in the same town as his parents, his aunt and uncle, and one of his cousins.

Living near your extended family can be a great gift. With scads of cousins, many attending the same school, our kids have a ready-made social group and instant acceptance. Constant family closeness can be cloying, however, so it's good to live "at least a bus ride away," as a friend of ours jokingly recommended.

In Search of Everlasting Love

When Is Being Close to Family Too Close?

Patrick (of Irish descent) and Esperanza (of Hispanic descent) were married three years and had one son, Johnny. Esperanza's family was very close knit, and her mother, Maria, happily took care of Johnny while Patrick and Esperanza worked. Patrick saw his mother-in-law nearly every day when he picked Johnny up after work. Other family members were usually there visiting and chatting, and Patrick was expected to stay awhile to say hello.

While grateful for his mother-in-law's help, Patrick felt uncomfortable with Esperanza's close and talkative family. He did not want to join in their gossip. Also, the family gathered together frequently at Baptisms, birthdays, weddings, holidays, and so forth. Patrick became so ill at ease that he began drinking heavily at family gatherings, and Esperanza's family objected. Esperanza still insisted it was rude for Patrick not to attend.

Through therapy, Patrick recognized that his pattern of turning to alcohol was ultimately making matters worse, and healthier coping mechanisms had worked successfully in the past. He committed to exercising before or after a family gathering to help manage stress. Esperanza, on the other hand, accepted that these functions were difficult for her introverted husband and explained to her family that sometimes he wanted to spend time alone after a hard workweek.

Reflection Questions

1. How did Patrick and Esperanza's different cultural backgrounds affect their expectations of involvement with in-laws and extended family?

2. Was it fair to expect Patrick to visit with his mother-in-law when he picked up his child from her house after work? How could he avoid joining in the gossip?

3. What's the best way for Esperanza to handle her family if they continue to object that Patrick doesn't spend enough time with them?

Manny's Diagnosis

In this situation, finding a workable compromise wasn't easy. Patrick was right not to want to join in gossip at his mother-in-law's house, and Esperanza was right that Patrick ought to spend time with her family. By putting each other's needs ahead of their own desires, however, the couple was able to resolve the conflict in a way that protected their marriage. Even if Esperanza's family objects in the short term, eventually they will understand—and knowing he's no longer obligated to attend every event will make it easier for Patrick to enjoy the ones he does attend.

Have the two of you decided on a family holiday schedule that works for you? Holiday madness is not always fun and can be especially difficult when families live far apart. Deciding who will travel and who will host, and how much of the family to include, takes careful planning. You might also want to set aside time to create new family traditions on your own. As the family increases in number, expect that the dynamics will change—and learn to see it as a good thing, as a chance to grow in love.

For many families, holiday dinners are among the most cherished memories, providing an invaluable opportunity to strengthen family ties. As Pope John Paul II stated, "Did Jesus not institute the Eucharist in a family-like setting during the Last Supper? When you meet for meals and are together in harmony, Christ is close to you" (*Letter to Families* [*LF*], 18). However, holiday meals can also be a lot of work!

As much as possible, give generously of your time and effort in helping to create these special family memories, as a way of investing in your new family's future. When we first got married, our parents still hosted most of the family dinners. But as our parents grew older, they began to expect the next generation to take over. This process happened in baby steps for us. The first holidays we hosted at our house involved us setting the table with the linen, china, crystal, and silver, with Mama Carmen doing all the cooking. Over the years, we began to take over the cooking as well as the table setting and cleaning up afterward.

As the family grew through marriage and childbirth, the task soon fell squarely on our shoulders to feed sixteen adults and thirteen children on three major holidays—Thanksgiving, Easter, and Christmas. We also threw birthday parties at home for each of our six kids, an Epiphany party for at least sixty people, plus celebrations for Mother's Day, Father's Day, the Fourth of July, and here or there a First Communion bash. While we loved these gatherings, soon it seemed we were always preparing or recovering from some family celebration. Something had to give.

First, we asked people to bring potluck dishes. "People don't do that in Spain" was the muttered objection, but we did it anyway. Then we dropped gentle hints about how the family could split up into separate groups at separate houses for the holiday celebrations. The hints went largely unheeded. Then we got mad.

One Thanksgiving, I got into a tense discussion with one of my sisters-in-law over how I felt the work was not being shared equally. "But you always say yes to having family dinners at your house," she said.

"Doesn't anyone feel obligated to reciprocate?" I asked.

"No!" she replied emphatically.

From my southern background of strictly enforced mutual hospitality, her reply made absolutely no sense. "For the next holiday," she suggested conspiratorially, "maybe you should just leave town."

So we did. Much to Oma and Opa's delight, we packed up our six kids and made the long drive from Long Island to spend an unscheduled Christmas in Virginia's lovely Shenandoah Valley. When we returned, Manny's cousins had the whole family over for New Year's.

For Easter that year, we didn't invite the whole extended family. We also didn't set any places at the table or make any kiddie food for the children. They ate Easter ham or candy, and we didn't check too closely to see which one they picked. My sister-in-law Elisa agreed to host a Mother's Day celebration at her house, since it fell on the same weekend as her son's First Communion. My sister-in-law Nancy agreed to host a joint First Communion party for her son and our daughter. And the next year my sister-in-law Marzena invited us for a small dinner party to say thanks for all the hosting we'd done. Manny happily remarked, "Change is good!" After all, the goal of family life is *mutual* service with everyone contributing what they can.

Holiday squabbles highlight the importance of learning how to communicate and resolve conflicts with all the members of the family, not just your spouse. The purpose is to forge that intimate community of life and love that John Paul II talked about. We don't choose our family members the way we choose our friends. We are bound to them through vows and blood (*FC*, 21).

"All members of the family, each according to his or her own gift, have the grace and responsibility of building, day by day, the communion of persons," stated John Paul II (*FC*, 21). This communion grows out of "an affinity of feelings, affections and interests" that is nurtured by constant effort and "preserved and perfected through a great spirit of sacrifice" by all family members (*CCC*, 2206; *FC*, 21). It also requires a "ready and generous openness . . . to understanding, to forbearance, to pardon, to reconciliation" (*FC*, 21). No one knows you like your family, which means no one needs to forgive you as much as your family.

Creating Loving Communion on a Worldwide Scale

Efforts to bond with extended family members should create an authentic community founded on an "ever deeper and more intense communion" (*FC*, 18). Because if we can't unite our own families, how will we ever fulfill the desire of Our Lord Jesus "that they may all be one" throughout the earth (Jn 17:21)?

The authentic, loving communion within our families should spread to encompass the entire human family. When we look at others, we see not strangers, competitors, or enemies but "in the baptized, the children of our mother the Church; in every human person, a son or daughter of the One who wants to be called 'our Father'" (CCC, 2212). The ability to recognize our relatedness to others begins within our own extended families.

The two of us have extended families that include Sevillanos, Madrilenos, Colombians, French-Moroccans, Poles, Argentineans, Egyptians, and Virginians. Our family members' religious affiliations range the gamut from Catholicism to Episcopalianism, Judaism, Coptic Orthodox, and former Muslim. Our families are truly a microcosm of the peoples of the earth. Through overcoming divisions and disharmonies within our own families, we hope to contribute in some small way to peace and understanding in our corner of the world.

Bonus Material

Conversation Starters

- How would you describe your process for deciding how much involvement your in-laws have in your married life?
- Can you remember a time when the two of you reached an impasse on this issue? How did you resolve it?
- How do you handle holidays? Do you see room for improvement?
- What do you believe is your responsibility toward both sets of your parents as they become elderly

or infirm? Have the two of you discussed this and reached an agreement?

Action Plan

Do something nice for your in-laws today. Send a note, give them a ride to the doctor, or take them a homemade treat if they live nearby. If they've helped you recently, say thank you. If they've given you good advice, acknowledge it. And then do the same for your own parents.

Catechism Corner

"Respect for parents . . . derives from *gratitude* toward those who, by the gift of life, their love and their work, have brought their children into the world and enabled them to grow in stature, wisdom, and grace" (*CCC*, 2215).

PART II

CALLED TO BE FREE

Wise Choices for Your Work, Money, and Spare Time

Freedom to marry means not being forced to the altar by people or circumstances, and not being barred by any law (*CCC*, 1625). But freedom within marriage means something different. It means freedom to love without counting the cost and without expecting anything in return. It means freedom to make the best and wisest choices for ourselves and the ones we love.

Our everyday choices can lead us closer to God and those who matter most to us, or further away from them. Our most important choices center on our most valuable resources: our work, money, and time. When we use these resources wisely, we're being good stewards.

Through work, we can use our talents to support ourselves and our families. We also have the opportunity to leave the world a better place than we found it. Discovering the divine value of even the littlest tasks we do can help us to balance what might feel like competing demands of God, family, and work.

We can also put our money to a higher use. Godly principles of money management are actually quite practical and can show us how to take care of our needs while helping the less fortunate as well.

Like our work and our money, our spare time is a precious asset. It's important to spend some of our spare time serving our friends and our communities. This way, we can use our freedom to make wise choices for the good of ourselves and others.

4.

Turning Meaningless Drudgery
into Meaningful Work

How to Prioritize God, Family, and Work

> Man must work out of regard for others, especially
> his own family, but also for the society he belongs
> to, . . . since he is the heir to the work of genera-
> tions and at the same time a sharer in building the
> future.
>
> —Pope John Paul II, *Laborem Exercens*, 16

When I met Manny, work was my top priority. I loved my
job as a New York City lawyer and spent Sunday afternoons tidying my office and getting mentally prepared for
the week ahead. Pleasing my family was also important
to me, and only after that did I concern myself with God.
Manny had the same priorities, only in the opposite order.
He placed God at the top of his priority list. Then came
family and, finally, work.

When I met Manny, my priorities gradually began to shift. Instead of going to the office on Sunday afternoons, I started going with him to Mass and dinner with Mama Carmen and José. And yet, the shift did not happen easily. It felt somehow disloyal to put my employer in third place. But I soon saw the wisdom of how Manny had ordered his priorities, and I began to challenge myself to achieve a more balanced lifestyle—a goal I continue to pursue each day now that I'm a work-at-home wife and mother!

No matter what job God calls us to undertake, he gives each of us the same twenty-four hours to accomplish everything we need to do. The Benedictines used to divide the day into three segments: eight hours for work, eight hours for prayer, and eight hours for rest. Married couples follow a different routine revolving around family life, providing for and nurturing the children they receive from the Lord, and tending to their own needs as well as that of extended family and friends.

The Catholic Work Ethic:
Work as a Blessing, Not a Burden

Catholicism regards work as a blessing and a source of human dignity. When God told Adam and Eve to "fill the earth and subdue it" (Gn 1:28), he gave them the mission to participate in the divine work of creation (see *Laborem Exercens* [LE], 25 and *CCC*, 2427). Although work became difficult and toilsome after our first parents left paradise, work is still "a good thing for man" because it's how he "*achieves fulfillment* as a human being" (*LE*, 9).

Whereas today's society categorizes people into white-collar and blue-collar workers, from a Catholic perspective, the value of our work does not depend on the type of job we have. By worshipping Jesus, who was a carpenter and a carpenter's son, Christianity turned notions of profession-based status on their heads (*LE*, 6). St. Josemaría Escrivá wrote, "It is time for us Christians to shout from the rooftops that work is a gift from God and that it makes no sense to classify men differently, according to their occupation, as if some jobs were nobler than others. Work, all work, bears witness to the dignity of man, to his dominion over creation."[1]

The primary purpose of our work is to obtain food, clothing, and shelter so we can survive (*LE*, 5). According to the *Catechism*, "Everyone should be able to draw from work the means of providing for his life and that of his family" (*CCC*, 2428). Stable, secure work—and the steady source of income it provides—make it possible for us to get married and start a family (*LE*, 10). Love for our families helps us see work as the blessing it was meant to be.

The Church leaves us free to choose the wisest work/life balance for our families. Our marriage is our vocation. Our daily work is a component of that vocation. It is how we live out our marriage as a sacrament of service and how we take care of those we love. Work takes many forms, such as earning money, changing diapers, writing prescriptions, and writing books. All are ways to support the family and follow the paths that God has prepared for us to walk in. If we work with a spirit of service and our eyes set on God, "there is no vocation more religious than work."[2]

Manny's Story: Working across Generations

My siblings and I once took a trip to visit my father's hometown in Spain, a small village nestled in the mountains of Huelva in the southern province of Andalusia. This is not the kind of place that gets many tourists, and I remember one time in particular with my siblings when we were surrounded by a group of tough-looking Spaniards. Tensions mounted—until one of them recognized us: "They're okay; their grandfather was the veterinarian." The mood lifted immediately. It didn't matter that my grandfather had been dead for more than two decades. We were the vet's grandkids.

That day I discovered how the investment of a life in a worthy endeavor can leave an impression that can span many generations. During the Spanish Civil War my grandfather had helped many people on both sides of the conflict. I remember him as a warm, easygoing, mild-mannered man who spoke in a whisper (his larynx had been removed due to cancer). He worked hard to care for his family and his community, a trait that came to characterize my father as well, who at seventy-six and in "semiretirement" still works more than forty hours each week in his practice. He considers it a privilege to assist other people.

I grew up believing that helping others is very important. I recall hearing stories about my maternal grandfather, Anastasio, who died when my mother was only twelve, leaving his wife to raise six young children in Spain during the harsh years that followed the Spanish Civil War. The youngest of his six children, Antonio, was only a baby when his father died. And yet he was able to attend university due to the sacrifices of his siblings. He went on to become a successful businessman as well as a loving husband and father, always willing to share his largesse with his siblings.

These stories inspire me. They are my heritage. And so, when I consider the question of work/life balance, I try to follow their example and repeat a mantra to sort out the particulars: "God, family, and work," in that order.

Even so, finding that balance can be a challenge. I need to earn a living, often working fifty to sixty hours a week.

While I would like to have dinner with my family every night, two nights a week I work late and arrive home to a quiet house in which even the mice are sleeping. So I make it a priority to be home for dinner at six on the other days. Although I previously commuted to a hospital in New York City, I recently began working part-time at a local Catholic hospital only ten minutes away from home. I also discontinued Saturday office hours in my private practice, giving our family a chance to spend more time together on the weekends.

Obviously, what works for Karee and I may not work for you. Each couple must approach the matter with the express understanding and expectation that you are each called to give 100 percent of yourself to the marriage. God first, family second, and work last; how you accomplish this is up to you.

Making Family-Friendly Career Choices

A crucial first step in building a successful career is finding a suitable job. A crucial first step in building a successful marriage is evaluating how that job will affect your home life. A "dream" job could turn into a nightmare if it constantly disrupts family life. Late nights and weekends, constant business travel, and canceled vacations can create tremendous conflict in a marriage, and an overly demanding job can turn work into unpleasant drudgery.

It's important for the two of you to sit down and, as a couple, list your priorities—the goals the two of you want to achieve through your family life. This will help you to find balance between the needs of the home and the needs of each individual. Everyone will have a different list, but here are some broad categories you might want to consider:

- *Location*: How much of a commute are you willing to handle? Fifteen minutes? Sixty minutes or more? Do you want to live near extended family members who could watch your children while you work?
- *Flexibility*: Do you want the flexibility to work from 7:00 a.m. to 3:00 p.m. instead of from 9:00 a.m. to 5:00 p.m.? Do you want to work at least part of the time from home?
- *Finances*: Do you want to live on one salary? If so, you might have to compromise on location or flexibility. Will your employer offer student loan forgiveness or pay for an advanced degree? If so, factor that into your salary comparison.
- *Parenting benefits*: Can you find an employer that offers paid maternity and paternity leave? What about an on-site corporate day-care center so you can visit the kids during your lunch hour?
- *Supportive work environment*: Do you want a work environment that supports your faith, such as a Catholic hospital, school, or publisher?

Finding family-friendly work takes on heightened importance during the parenting years.

Women and Work

Women often struggle to achieve work/life balance, especially when they have young children at home. The question of whether to work outside the home, to work from home, or to be the primary, unpaid homemaker and caretaker of young children frequently tops the list of tough decisions facing wives and mothers. The unique needs and circumstances of each family can make it difficult to determine what is best. And yet, the woman who prioritizes God first, family second, and work last can be confident that God will show her the right path.

Moms who choose to stay at home use their God-given talents for an important mission. John Paul II declared, "How important and burdensome is *the work women do within the family unit. That work should be acknowledged and deeply appreciated.* The 'toil' of a woman who, having given birth to a child, nourishes and cares for that child and devotes herself to its upbringing, particularly in the early years, is so great as to be comparable to any professional work" (*LF*, 17).

And yet, many devout Catholic women—including many saints—have used their gifts outside the home in a variety of capacities. St. Gianna Molla, for example, worked as a doctor while raising four children.[3] St. Margaret of Scotland had eight children, devoted much time to serving the poor, and founded several churches, all while reigning as Queen of Scotland (*Lives . . . of the Saints for Every Day of the Year* [*LS*], 475). (Given her position, though, Queen Margaret probably had a little help.)

By sharing their talents and gifts with the world, women working outside the home bring a distinctively feminine "genius" to the wider community. In his 1995 *Letter to Women*, John Paul II proclaimed, "Thank you, women who work! You are present and active in every area of life—social, economic, cultural, artistic and political. In this way you make an indispensable contribution to the growth of a culture which unites reason and feeling . . . [and] to the establishment of economic and political structures ever more worthy of humanity."[4]

Fortunately, decisions about how and where to work can change over time depending on the family's circumstances.

In Search of Everlasting Love

How Do Moms Decide Whether to Reenter the Workforce?

Martha worked as a lawyer for ten years before having children. Then she and her husband, Mick, had three children in three years. Martha thought it was important to stay home during the children's formative years, and so for five years she remained at home while Mick worked as an architect.

Although they could live off of one income, Martha decided to return to work part-time once the children all reached an age to attend school. She worked for the Legal Aid Society, providing free legal services for the indigent and underserved. From her perspective, representing the poor was using her God-given talents for an important and necessary mission. She felt that work gave her a break from the children, and the children gave her a break from work.

Reflection Questions

1. What factors did Martha balance in reaching the decision to return to work?
2. How do you think her choices affected her family?
3. Can you see yourself making a similar decision?

Manny's Diagnosis

Although many moms reenter the workforce for financial reasons, money wasn't Martha's primary motivation. Instead, Martha balanced her children's needs for her care with her desire to use her education and experience to serve others. By working part-time while the children attended school,

Martha attempted to minimize any negative impact her job might have on the family. Some moms feel guilty going back to work, but Martha's personal sense of fulfillment made her more willing and able to serve the children's needs when they were at home.

Career decisions like Martha's often require careful thought, and turning to God in prayer can help us make the wisest choice.

Working for the Kingdom: Are You Listening for the Call?

Prayer can be an invaluable aid in discerning and achieving our professional goals. When our friend Frank started looking for work in a very bad economy, he began praying a novena (a nine-day prayer) to St. Jude, the patron saint of hopeless causes. After Frank found work, he kept praying to St. Jude every day in order to keep the job he had and get an even better one.

Not everybody who prays a novena gets a job, of course. Finding work also requires a large investment of elbow grease. In my third and last year of law school, I applied for nearly a dozen judicial clerkships and hundreds of law firm jobs. Ultimately, I received only one offer for a clerkship and one offer from a law firm. Both employers were located in New York City, the last place I ever wanted to live. Needless to say, I moved to New York, where I met my husband, converted to Catholicism, and had a passel of kids. God made it obvious what path he wanted me to follow by eliminating any other alternatives!

Not all choices are so clear. When work and life get out of balance, it can be excruciatingly difficult to find the right solution, especially if we don't ask God to show us the way.

–––––––––––––––––––––––– 🗝━◯ ––––––––––––––––––––––––

In Search of Everlasting Love

*What Should You Do If Work and
Life Are Out of Balance?*

James was a highly successful Wall Street investment broker. Because he had many clients in Japan, his business hours didn't even begin until 7:00 p.m. (EST). Mariko, his wife, was born and raised in Japan, so she understood and didn't complain about James's long working hours and unusual schedule.

When James's Japanese clients visited the United States, he had to wine and dine them. Stress combined with the constant presence of alcohol led James to begin abusing alcohol. He noticed that he was losing control, but Mariko showed little sympathy.

Eventually reaching the breaking point, James quit his job before he had a new one. Furious, Mariko contemplated moving back to Japan with the children and without James. James struggled to recover from his stressful working conditions and his incipient alcohol addiction.

Three months later, James found a new job that did not require him to entertain clients as much, and their marital difficulties abated. However, both James and Mariko came to see that the whole situation had damaged their marriage.

Reflection Questions

1. How could prayer and communication have helped James and Mariko to head off the crisis?

2. How could Mariko have reacted differently both before and after James quit his job?

3. How can the couple repair their relationship now?

Manny's Diagnosis

Through prayer, James and Mariko might have been able to recognize James's problem as a family problem and bring it to God together rather than both of them expecting James to find the right solution by himself. James's job transition could have happened much more smoothly and with less harm to the marriage had Mariko understood and supported the change. James and Mariko can repair their relationship by committing to discerning their future path together with God's help so that other potential changes do not catch them so unprepared.

Doing Your "Home" Work

For the sake of harmony in the home, it's good to recognize that work inside the walls of the home deserves at least as much effort as work outside the home. Taking care of the house and children, while incredibly rewarding, requires full attention to a seemingly endless list of chores.

Chore distribution depends upon numerous variables, and every family needs to do what works for them. Some spouses divide work by location—our friend Cathy does all the work on the interior of the house, and her husband does all the work on the exterior of the house, including the gardens. Another friend does all the decorating, like pillows and curtains, while her husband fixes the innards of things, like plumbing, wiring, and carpentry. Dividing up the household chores depends on each spouse's work schedule, their preferences, and their expectations going into the marriage based on how they were raised.

I grew up in a home where my parents worked together on daily chores, while in Manny's family this was his mother's domain. Naturally, finding a system that worked for us required some give and take. Gender roles have blurred over the years, and very few household responsibilities remain exclusively male or female (although Manny holds firm on the recommendation that garbage removal, barring extraordinary circumstances, is a man's job).

Both Manny and I like to cook, so I cook on weeknights and Manny takes over on weekends. He makes pancakes on Saturday or Sunday mornings, just as Opa did when I was a little girl. The pancake-making tradition is not only messy but also a great deal of fun for the kids who pitch in to help. Barbeques are also generally within Manny's domain, and he seems to delight in the practice and execution of lighting the fire and burning all sorts of food upon it in order to feed his family. Finding an equitable chore distribution didn't happen instantaneously, however.

Early in our marriage, I adopted my parents' methods without really thinking about it. For example, I folded Manny's laundry and laid it on top of his dresser for him to put away, just as Opa always had. Manny took this as an affront and sniped at me, interpreting my action as reluctance to carry a loving act to its conclusion, since his mother not only folded the laundry but also placed it in the drawers. Miffed, I decided to leave the laundry on his dresser anyway . . . and the pile of clean socks grew alarmingly high.

The standoff eventually led to a discussion and, rather than bickering about who was right and who was wrong, we both acknowledged that we were being obstinate and inflexible. Understanding Manny's perspective once he explained it, I conceded the battle and put the socks *in* his dresser drawer, since it wasn't that much harder than laying them on the dresser top. There's no point in prolonging a silly fight through stubbornness or clinging to our parents' patterns when they aren't adapting easily to our new life. Nowadays, Manny and I both recognize how hard it is to keep a large household running, and we try to express our gratitude for all that the other does.

On Working Well

Both inside and outside the home, "a Catholic layman or laywoman is someone who takes work seriously," said John Paul II.[5] Our work deserves our best efforts during the hours we've chosen to devote to it. God is not satisfied with shoddy workmanship.[6]

Workmanship is not measured by skill alone. The value of our work can be measured by the love and care we put into it. Even the smallest, most mundane task can be a kind of offering to God. Just look up from your work and think silently, "My Lord, this is for you." Ask yourself, "Am I doing at this moment what I ought to be doing?" and revive your enthusiasm and prayerful intent. St. Paul explained how each of us can turn ordinary work into a quest for heaven: "Whatever your task, put yourselves into it, as done for the Lord and not for your masters, since you know that from the Lord you will receive the inheritance as your reward" (Col 3:23–24).

When possible, use visual aids to remind yourself that God is ultimately the boss of you. One of our Spanish cousins carries a small crucifix with him to place on his desk at work. A stay-at-home-mom friend has pictures of Our Lady in every room in her house to remind her of the deeper meaning of her daily chores. In her daily calendar, our friend Kristin writes a set of initials next to each event or item on her to-do list. These initials represent the name of someone close to her who needs her prayers. As she accomplishes the ordinary tasks of her day, she tries to keep in mind that her efforts are a type of prayer for those people she loves.

"Work is for man, not man for work" (*LE*, 6). In other words, the person who does the work and the person who is served by that work are both more important than the work itself (*CCC*, 2428). Work is therefore not "*what* you do as much as it is *whom* you serve," according to mom blogger and author Jennifer Fulwiler. Finding your vocation "is simply a matter of discerning whom you'll serve and how you'll serve them."[7]

When you see the smile that you put on someone's face, you know you have served him or her well. But work also serves the entire community, even people we will never meet (*CCC*, 2428). Work is how we "contribute to the continual advance of science and technology" and improve "the cultural and moral level of the society" in which we live (*LE*, introduction). God gave us our talents not only to benefit ourselves but also to serve our neighbors and society as a whole.

We don't work just because we have to or because it's interesting. We work because we have a moral obligation to make the world a better place. In the words of John Paul II, "Man must work out of regard for others, especially his own family, but also for the society he belongs to . . . since he is the heir to the work of generations and at the same time a sharer in building the future. . . . All this constitutes the moral obligation of work" (*LE*, 16).

Through our work, we help fill the material and spiritual needs of others. Regardless of our profession, our work will introduce us to people with whom we can share the Good News. When we were both working and living in Manhattan, Manny and I always invited our coworkers to hear our church choir sing. My secretary, who was Jewish, attended a Holy Week service called Tenebrae and said she truly loved the somber ritual of it. Manny's friend from work, a Jew-turned-Buddhist, also frequently came to Mass to hear our choir.

Don't be ashamed to take your faith with you to the workplace—it's an integral part of you. "Have you ever bothered to think," queried St. Josemaría, "how absurd it is to leave one's Catholicism aside on entering a university, or a professional association, . . . or Congress, as if you were checking your hat at the door?" (*TW*, 353). By placing God first on our priority list, we invite God to be a part of our working life, not just our worshipping life. And with God's help, our faith will make us better workers and our work will lead us to grow in faith.

Bonus Material

Conversation Starters

- What priority does work have in your life?
- What led you to choose your particular work or career?
- Do you struggle to balance home life and work life?
- How did your parents balance home life and work life? Will that model work for you?

Action Plan

Remember that your work is your way of being God's hands active in the world. Pick one way mentioned in the previous section to infuse your work with prayer, enthusiasm, and care for the people you are serving. Then make a habit of it!

Catechism Corner

"Work honors the Creator's gifts and the talents received from him. . . . By enduring the hardship of work in union with Jesus, the carpenter of Nazareth and the one crucified on Calvary, man . . . shows himself to be a disciple of Christ" (CCC, 2427).

5.

Turning Ownership into Stewardship

> Once man begins to lose sight of a God who loves
> him . . . earthly life becomes nothing more than
> the scenario of a battle for existence, of a desperate
> search for gain, and financial gain before all else.
> —Pope John Paul II, *Letter to Families*, 19

Money is only a means to an end. It's an aid to survival, comfort, generous living, and building up a better society as well as God's kingdom. But if our whole lives center around money—earning it, spending it, or saving it—then we fall into a trap of our own making. Money becomes our master.

An attitude of stewardship can set us free. Good stewardship recognizes that everything we have comes from God, even the talents and opportunities that enable us to earn a living. God gives us these things so we can use them for his glory, not just accomplish our own personal goals. As the *Catechism* tells us, all owners are in reality stewards who have the task of making their property fruitful and sharing the benefits with others, first of all their family (CCC, 2404).

When we think of money as "ours" rather than "mine" and "yours," it is easier to make shared financial decisions for the good of the whole family. On the other hand, nothing destroys a marriage faster than a me-first attitude. In his first papal visit to the United States, John Paul II warned us that "the great danger for family life, in the midst of any society whose idols are pleasure, comfort and independence, lies in the fact that people close their hearts and become selfish."[1]

By changing our attitude from "me thinking" to "we thinking," we become more grateful for what each spouse brings to the marriage. When we consider the "big picture" financial needs of the family and control our own impulsive spending in order to better meet those needs, we become more responsible. Our hearts stay centered on our family, not our finances.

Manny taught me the importance of this we-centered attitude early in our relationship. When the law firm where I worked increased my salary until it was above what Manny earned as a medical resident, I was terrified that his masculinity would feel threatened. Instead, he grinned and said, "We got a raise!"

By moving from a me-centered to a we-centered and a God-centered vision of finances, spouses can become good stewards, as united in money matters as they are in all other aspects of their lives together. With this stewardship attitude in mind, let's turn to the daily nitty-gritty of marital finances. We have found six tips that can help to make your finances trouble free:

1. Talk to each other.
2. Establish joint financial priorities.
3. Plan wisely.
4. Save for your family's future.
5. Tithe or donate a fixed percentage of your income.
6. Pay your taxes. (Yes, really!)

Let's take each of these one at a time.

Tip 1: Talk to Each Other

Patients in therapy will frequently spill all the details of their sexual lives but then clam up when it's time to start talking about money. For some reason, most people feel very embarrassed and reluctant to discuss money. Spouses are no exception, as the following case study shows.

In Search of Everlasting Love

Can Financial Miscommunication Destroy a Marriage?

Carlos came to therapy seeking help with his marriage. A devout Catholic who worked in the financial industry, Carlos appeared both confident and intelligent. He and his wife, Mary, had four children, and she was staying home to raise them. Carlos saw his role in the marriage as that of the provider, describing himself disparagingly as a "human ATM." He commuted more than four hours daily in order to provide for his family. He felt bitter, angry, and used.

Carlos's wife seemed warm and cheerful but unaware of the financial pressures on her husband. She said things started going downhill when Carlos accepted a new business venture, requiring them to pull up stakes and move to another state. When Carlos's new business venture failed, he took a different job with an onerous commute in order to pay the mortgage and maintain their lifestyle. Tired and irritable, he grew impatient over seemingly small matters such as their kids leaving shoes around the house. Mary consoled herself largely by shopping, which only exacerbated their money problems. Carlos retreated into an unhealthy cycle of brooding silence and explosive anger. Soon he and Mary became unable to discuss a rational solution to their money problems. Eventually, she filed for divorce . . . and learned to limit her spending when the judge set a fixed amount for alimony and child support.

Reflection Questions

1. Why did Carlos keep working for a job that required him to be on the road commuting more than four hours a day?

2. Why did Mary continue shopping when it hurt the family financially?

3. How could better communication have helped to avoid the disintegration of their marriage?

Manny's Diagnosis

Carlos wanted to be a good provider for his family, and failed to see how his behavior placed great emotional stress on them, stress that Mary relieved by spending money rather than confronting her husband directly. Carlos downplayed the enormous pressure he was under, not wanting to admit he simply couldn't continue to provide enough income to keep up with the family's inflated spending levels. Because both Mary and Carlos were unable to express to each other the issues at the heart of their conflict, the family was torn apart. In contrast, when couples make open and honest communication a priority early in their relationship, it sets a positive course for their married lives.

Sadly, many couples avoid talking about money matters before the wedding, as we learned from teaching pre-Cana. As part of our marriage preparation course, we would hand out a questionnaire designed to find out how many important issues the couple had talked about and agreed on. A score of 100 percent in a particular category meant the couple had discussed and reached agreement on all the key issues. In the finances category, couples rarely received a score higher than 25 percent. In most cases, they just hadn't talked about it.

One remarkable couple scored in the eightieth or ninetieth percentile. How? After he and his fiancée decided to get married, the groom simply "opened the books" to her. (This of course presupposes that you've kept track of your finances well enough that there are "books" to open!)

Even if you don't keep meticulous financial records, you likely have some degree of financial self-knowledge about the following items:

- the amount of money in your paycheck
- the amount you spend on rent and other set expenses whether you have savings or debts
- whether any money is left over at the end of the month

Sharing these basic facts about your financial circumstances will prevent unpleasant surprises after the wedding—and will also help you both make prudent choices about your wedding budget, or any other large-ticket item (such as a home or a college account).

Another good thing to share is your financial habits. Do you regularly put money into savings or retirement accounts? How much do you give to the Church or other charitable organizations? How much debt do you keep on your credit cards? How often do you eat out? Do you regularly send money to support other members of your family? Do you spend money on hobbies such as music lessons or athletic clubs that you feel are important to your personal development? Do you expect these habits to continue, perhaps indefinitely, after marriage?

Answers to these questions will help you identify issues you still need to discuss and about which you need to reach agreement—understanding, of course, that such discussions must continue throughout the marriage as circumstances change. Allow love, not money, to be the guiding principle of your relationship, and show respect for each other even when discussing difficult subjects such as finances. Love doesn't engage in name calling, eye rolling, or door slamming. Ask God to help you become good stewards of the gifts he has entrusted to you and to show you how to communicate with charity about marital finances.

Tip 2: Establish Joint Financial Priorities

With rare exceptions, married couples don't usually fight over how much money they have. They fight over how they spend it. Learning not only to discuss but also to reach consensus on how you spend your money is an important milestone in your long-term happiness.

Jake and Judy's story illustrates how easy it is to fight over money when couples haven't set joint priorities.

In Search of Everlasting Love

Do Financial Goals Sometimes Interfere with
Relationship Goals?

Money was tight for Jake and Judy, but they managed to make ends meet. One day, Jake decided to surprise Judy with a beautiful gemstone necklace. Instead of happily accepting the gift, Judy became upset and returned the jewelry to the store, leaving her husband feeling angry and embarrassed. Jake didn't understand why Judy was so upset.

Judy saw herself as the money manager of their household. It was her job to take their income and stretch it to fit their expenses. Jake, like many men, assumed that all women, including his wife, would love to receive expensive jewelry. Yet when Jake bought his wife expensive jewelry, he actually hurt her ability to manage the family finances. She valued things for the home and family far more than luxuries for herself. Instead of pleasing Judy, the gift upset her.

What Judy didn't stop to consider is what Jake was trying to say with this extravagant gift. Perhaps he wanted to give her a symbol of his ability to provide for his family. Maybe he heard her admire a friend's necklace and wanted her to have a similar luxury. When Judy rejected his gift, Jake felt Judy was rejecting him.

Reflection Questions

1. How does this conflict reveal Jake and Judy's different attitudes about "little luxuries" and how money should be spent?

2. How could they have handled the situation better?

3. Has your relationship ever encountered a similar conflict?

Manny's Diagnosis

Judy thought little luxuries were a waste of money, but Jake thought they were a sign of love and a reward for hard work. If Jake had asked Judy before buying the necklace, she could have suggested gifts that would have made her happier and fit better with her financial priorities. If Judy had talked to Jake before returning the jewelry to the store, they could have exchanged the necklace together and purchased a gift that pleased them both. By acting together, this couple could have invested not just in a necklace but also in their future happiness.

As Jake and Judy's story shows, spouses don't automatically have the same financial priorities. They may start by placing different priorities on paying off debt, saving for a house or car, and donating to charitable organizations. Developing a unified approach requires a lot of communication and compromise in order to determine what's most important to both spouses.

While couples should set their priorities jointly, one spouse will usually be better suited to handle day-to-day details such as paying bills. I do that for my family. Our friend Christina does that for her family as well. We have both found, however, how important it is to keep our husbands involved. When Christina's husband complained they were spending too much money, she invited him to pay the bills with her. They discovered a lot of unnecessary credit card expenses to cut back on.

Keeping the principles of stewardship in mind and remembering that our ultimate hope is in heaven, not in a fat bank account, helps to cut down the friction that can arise in trying to set and attain joint financial goals. Manny and I are blessed to have a very concrete reminder of our joint stewardship responsibilities. At our wedding ceremony, we incorporated a Spanish custom in which the priest blessed a small basket of gold coins with biblical quotations on them. Then the priest poured the coins into Manny's hands. Manny poured them into my hands, I poured them into Manny's hands, and he returned them to the priest. The ritual symbolized that all Manny had was mine, all I had was his, and all we had was God's. We would hold nothing back from each other or from God, and money would be no exception.

Tip 3: Plan Wisely

Once you've agreed on your financial priorities, develop a plan to help achieve them. Jesus himself praised financial forethought, saying, "For which of you, intending to build a tower, does not first sit down and estimate the cost, to see whether he has enough to complete it? Otherwise, when he . . . is not able to finish, all who see it will begin to ridicule him" (Lk 14:28–29).

A good plan or budget should cover all your needs and some of your wants. St. Paul reminds us that our basic needs are simple: "For we brought nothing into the world, so that we can take nothing out of it; but if we have food and clothing, we will be content with these" (1 Tm 6:7–8). Modern families generally also require money for housing, furniture, utilities, medical and dental care, insurance, education, and transportation. And yet most of us easily confuse *needs* and *wants*.

This lesson can take a while to sink in. For example, before getting married, I assumed that every child *needed* his or her own room. A few years later, when our two kids filled our two available bedrooms, we decided to build an addition to our home for our next baby. "Can you afford it?" asked my parents. "Oh, that's not the issue," I assured them. "We *need* it." Then the architect gave us a ballpark estimate for the cost of the addition. It was appallingly high. My perceived need for an addition on the house quickly evaporated. And our kids seem remarkably happy to share their rooms.

We've also learned it's possible to live without the newest appliances, cars, and electronic gadgets. We don't buy a new appliance until the old one breaks, a habit we learned from our friends Sabrina and Joe. We hold on to our cell phones and computers until several generations of new technology have passed, for the simple reason that they still work fine. Why throw something away simply because it is old when it still retains value and usefulness? It is better to make do with what you have, which often means making do with less. "Don't forget it," advised St. Josemaría, "he has most who needs least. Don't create needs for yourself" (*TW*, 630).

A budget helps show us what we truly need. If we can't afford it, then in most cases we don't need it. Creating a budget requires an honest, thorough, and sometimes painful evaluation of our financial state. But it's an essential step in prudently managing the resources you share as a family. Helping you develop a budget is beyond the scope of this book, but several excellent books and computer programs exist to help you do it. We recommend just picking one and getting started.

By budgeting wisely, you can more easily follow these two key principles for financial happiness: (1) spend less than you earn and (2) don't spend money that you don't have. These principles can help you avoid debt like high credit card balances, for example. Credit cards can be useful if you pay off your balance in full every month, but interest rates for credit card debt are notoriously high and can eat up a budget. The next time you're tempted to spend more than you have, remember, "The borrower is the slave of the lender" (Prv 22:7).

Tip 4: Save for Your Family's Future

In the Old Testament, Joseph recommended that the Pharaoh of Egypt save 20 percent of the land's produce for seven good years so Egypt could survive through the next seven years of famine (see Gn 41:34–36).

This is a good lesson for all of us. You never know when years of famine might come. Whether it's an emergency fund to cushion the family against an unforeseen catastrophe or a retirement account to provide for your golden years, saving for the future is an important line item on any budget.

We keep three to six months' living expenses in our emergency fund, in case Manny loses his job unexpectedly. When necessary, we dip into that fund for major cash purchases. Also, we try to invest up to 10 percent of our annual income in tax-sheltered retirement accounts. Depending on the year, it's not always possible to save that much. But we always have an eye to the future.

Part of our savings is invested in a Catholic mutual fund, which does not purchase shares in companies involved in abortion or pornography or in companies with antifamily policies that undermine the Sacrament of Matrimony. For us, this helps to strike the proper balance between the right to seek a reasonable return to benefit our family and our desire to invest in morally acceptable activities.[2]

Unfortunately, the vast majority of Americans fail to save at all. Some are too poor, some are too burdened with debt, and some have an overly optimistic view of the future. But almost everyone can start by saving something, while working to overcome the obstacles that keep them from saving more.

Tip 5: Tithe

In addition to saving for our future needs, we should also help provide for the present needs of others. The Old Testament asked God's people to donate a tithe, which literally means a tenth: "Bring the full tithe into the storehouse, so that there may be food in my house, and thus put me to the test, says the LORD of hosts; see if I will not open the windows of heaven for you and pour down for you an overflowing blessing" (Mal 3:10).

While the Church doesn't require anyone to give a full 10 percent of his or her income, we do have an obligation to donate what we can to serve the material needs of the Church and the poor. As Jesus said, "Whoever has two coats must share with anyone who has none; and whoever has food must do likewise" (Lk 3:11).

My parents always took their responsibility to give to others very seriously. Although they were very thrifty, they always put money in the collection plate. I remember being astonished at the amounts written on the checks that Opa gave on Sunday mornings. But charitable giving is much more than an obligation or responsibility. Each person should freely give, "not reluctantly or under compulsion, for God loves a cheerful giver" (2 Cor 9:7). Giving from the heart actually helps us grow closer to God: "God doesn't want us to give because he needs our money; he wants us to give so that our hearts can grow. When we give, we remember that all we have comes from God and that we're completely dependent on Him. We grow in humility, trust, and gratitude, and our love of God and neighbor grows more consistent. . . . We give because we love."[3]

We should give not only because it's a good thing to do but also because it's the right thing to do. As St. John Chrysostom explained, God "gives to some people more than they need, not that they can enjoy great luxury, but to make them stewards on behalf of orphans, the sick, and the crippled."[4]

If you can't manage current expenses or save for your family's future, you might find the idea of tithing overwhelming. Consider donating your time and talent as part of your contribution or starting with a percentage less than a full 10 percent. Our parish recommends giving half your donations to the Church and the other half to the charity of your choice, either a reputable national organization or a local ministry in your community. By moderating your own wants and putting your own financial house in order, you will have more to share with others in need.

Tip 6: Pay Your Taxes

When the Pharisees asked Jesus whether it was lawful to pay taxes to Caesar, Jesus told them to "render therefore to Caesar the things that are Caesar's, and to God the things that are God's" (Mt 22:21 RSV). The *Catechism* echoes this sentiment, explaining that our duty to obey legitimate political authority requires us to pay our taxes (*CCC*, 2240).

There is no sin in taking all the legitimate tax deductions and exemptions possible, of course. People who own houses, have children, or donate to charity all receive tax breaks because the government wants to encourage this behavior. Lowering your taxes helps you to take good financial care of your family. On the other hand, outright tax evasion amounts to theft (*CCC*, 2409).

By paying what we owe in taxes, we contribute to the common good by providing the protection, resources, and services we all need—including those least able to pay for them. Tax revenues are crucially important in caring for the poorest and weakest members of society.[5] In 2014 there were more than 46.7 million people living in poverty in our country, according to the US Census Bureau.[6] Although most people don't like to pay taxes, contributing toward public services for those in need is a virtuous act; feel good about it!

Pray and Trust in God's Providence

None of the six tips we've detailed is guaranteed to erase financial adversity from your life. The Lord giveth and the Lord taketh away, as the Old Testament character Job said (see Jb 1:21). So our final piece of advice on finances is don't forget to pray. Jesus himself encouraged us to pray: "Give us this day our daily bread" (Mt 6:11). Prayer reminds us that everything we have comes from God, and we are only stewards.

The truth that God governs our financial destinies was hard for me to internalize. It took several brain tumors for me to get the point, in fact. After Manny was diagnosed with his third and then fourth brain tumor, it was no longer possible to pretend that the tumors were finally gone and never coming back. Among my many anxieties, I wondered how to support the children and myself if Manny died.

Prayer brought me to the realization that I had never truly trusted in God to provide. In my twenties, I relied on myself and my talents. When marriage and motherhood taught me how little I could accomplish on my own, I began to rely heavily on my husband. But I never gave God credit for giving me my talents or for sending me my wonderful husband. Not recognizing God as the source of all we had, I had no confidence in God to provide for the future through whatever opportunities he might send my way.

It took repeated crises in our married lives for me fully to accept the gospel passage that we chose for our wedding Mass: "Therefore do not worry, saying, 'What will we eat?' or 'What will we drink?' or 'What will we wear?' For . . . your heavenly Father knows that you need all these things. But strive first for the kingdom of God and his righteousness, and all these things will be given to you as well" (Mt 6:31–34).

When we have done all we can, leaving the rest in God's hands will bring us peace.

Bonus Material

Conversation Starters

- Do you and your spouse have different spending and saving patterns? How different are they?
- Are you comfortable discussing finances with each other, or does it sometimes cause conflict?
- How important do you think donating to charity is? Which charities do you support?
- How often do you pray about any financial worries you might have?

Action Plan

Together with your spouse, choose one of the tips from this chapter that you would like to put into action. Make a list of concrete steps to achieve your goal, and write those steps down on your calendar. Then make sure to follow up!

Catechism Corner

"The ownership of any property makes its holder a steward of Providence, with the task of making it fruitful and communicating its benefits to others, first of all his family" (CCC, 2404).

6.

Turning Inaction into Action

FAMILIES AT THE SERVICE OF OTHER FAMILIES

It is not in soul-searching or constant introspection that we encounter the Lord. . . . The power of grace . . . comes alive and flourishes to the extent that we, in faith, go out and give ourselves and the Gospel to others.

—Pope Francis, Holy Thursday Homily, March 28, 2013

Our friends Susan and Jerry, parents of five, include their children in their visits to Catholic Worker houses, which offer hospitality and support to the poor and homeless. During one visit, a resident named Jim complimented their infant son, so Susan and Jerry offered to place their baby boy in Jim's arms for a hug. When Jim protested, the baby flung wide his little arms and smiled expectantly. Gathering the baby to his burly chest, Jim began to cry. "No one has ever trusted me with a baby before," he said. Sharing your children and your family as part of your service to others can amount to a priceless gift.

The Church has established great charitable organizations throughout the ages, including networks of hospitals, schools, and orphanages. But families have their own role to play. "Families are meant to contribute to the transformation of the earth and the renewal of the world, of creation and of all humanity," stated John Paul II (*LF*, 18).

Families can transform the world simply by being who they are. Children who grow up in a loving family naturally learn how to share, communicate, settle differences, and value each person's equal dignity. Being a good family member prepares them to be a good member of society (*CCC*, 2207).

Parents can also teach their children from a young age that being a good member of society and a good Christian must be translated into concrete action. Concrete action taken for the benefit of others can bind a family together to a goal larger than themselves. It is important for families to speak up for their rights within the political sphere. Issues such as education, public housing, the minimum wage, unemployment benefits, legal protection of the marriage bond, and freedom to profess our religion all have an impact on families (see *CCC*, 2211). The Church can't and won't directly intervene in partisan politics. It's the responsibility of ordinary laypeople to participate in shaping the laws of their country (*CCC*, 2442). If families don't fight for their principles at the ballot box, they "will be the first victims of the evils that they have done no more than note with indifference" (*FC*, 44).

Some families have more time to devote to charitable activities than others. The priest who instructed us in pre-Cana warned us not to do the good we are not called to do. A couple came to this priest for counseling because the wife was attending many prayer groups and church-sponsored activities, but the husband wanted her to spend more time at home. The wife felt she was doing the right thing because she was serving the Church. The priest told the wife that her vocation was to be with her husband because her primary path to holiness was through her family.

One of the most important ways to serve the Church is *with* your family, as this next story demonstrates.

In Search of Everlasting Love

How Can Community Service Draw Families Closer Together?

Lily and Steve approached the parenting of their only child, Bobby, in very different ways. Lily thought Steve had an emotionally distant, hands-off style of parenting, while Steve believed he was simply encouraging his son's independence. Lily was more protective of Bobby, always wanting to keep close tabs on what he was doing; yet her husband felt she was sometimes overprotective.

Because of her husband's emotional distance, Lily poured a lot of energy into the mother-son bond. As Bobby entered his teen years, however, he wanted to assert his independence from his parents. They decided community service was a good way to help their son establish relationships in their faith community and help the family members to get closer by working toward a common goal.

Every couple of months, Lily, Steve, and Bobby spent a day packing food donations for the Franciscan Friars of the Renewal, an order dedicated to serving the poor. During these community service days, the family worked together without competing over who was in charge. They were all united in their mission to serve.

Reflection Questions

1. How did community service help Lily and Steve put their own problems in perspective?

2. Why was it easier for Lily and Steve to interact with their son at a charity event?

3. How did Steve's participation affect the family?

Manny's Diagnosis

Seeing the real-life challenges of poverty helped Lily and Steve put into perspective their own problems and parenting challenges. When the family participated together in the charity event, the event organizers were in control, so the family's interaction never turned into a power struggle. Steve's agreement to join in a day of community service for the sake of the family expressed his love for Lily and Bobby in deeds even when he was uncomfortable expressing it in words. Lily and Steve's example shows how including children in our community service efforts can benefit our own families in addition to benefiting others.

What if your family seems too busy or disinterested to participate regularly in charitable projects outside the home? Think of ways to weave charitable acts into the fabric of your daily life—beginning within the walls of your home.

Welcome Others into Your Home

A deeply personal way to serve your neighbors is by welcoming them into your home. Our friend Tony's father was a butcher, so the family always had enough to eat, even when other people in the community didn't. Tony's parents regularly made extra for dinner so anybody could come over and share in the family meal without feeling they were asking for a handout.

Hospitality has value even when it's not directed at the poorest of the poor. It strengthens the bonds among community members and encourages them to lend a helping hand when there's a new baby in the family, a recent death, or illness. It also turns neighbors into friends. One priest advised, "You should have people in and out of your house all day long. Your house should be a place that people want to spend time in." His theory was that the more friends we have, the more people we can share our love of Christ with.

So when we first moved to our house in the suburbs, we decided to reach out to our neighbors by throwing an annual Epiphany party for them. Around January 6 every year, we drop Los Reyes Magos (Feast of the Three Kings) invitations in the mailboxes of everyone on the block, even if we haven't met them yet and don't know their names. The invitations simply say, "To our neighbors." Kids are always encouraged to come. We sing Christmas carols to the accompaniment of an electric piano, a harmonica, or even a karaoke machine. We share our culture, food, and religion with as many as eighty of our neighbors, nourishing them both physically and spiritually.

For years, I also ran a book club for mothers in our home. The group chose books that would help strengthen our relationships with our families and with God. In an area where "grown-up" activities normally exclude children, one of the book club's most important rules was that moms could always bring their babies with them.

Following Mama Carmen and José's example that is typical in Spanish-speaking countries, we also opened our home for relatives to live with us. A couple of summers, we hosted young female cousins from Spain who came to the United States to learn English and see the sights. A male cousin stayed with us for almost an entire year while completing his postdoctoral fellowship in a hospital in New York City.

You can open your home the way we did or you can do it your own way by hosting small dinner parties or frequent play dates. But offering the hospitality of your own home is a simple and often very enjoyable way to show your neighbor the love of Christ.

Serve Your Community by Your Deeds

You don't have to go far out of your way to show kindness to a neighbor. Our friend Beth, a mother of six, earned our lasting gratitude from simple acts such as sending over a home-cooked meal or picking up a few extra grocery items when we had just brought a newborn baby home from the hospital.

Carpooling is another easy and common way that families serve other families in their community. We've been blessed by the generous help of many parents who have driven our children back and forth to extracurricular activities together with their own kids. They've rarely ever asked us to reciprocate—a good thing, since with six kids of our own we had very little room left in our car to take extra passengers.

Handing down kids' clothes and other baby-related paraphernalia is also very helpful. Our friends Connie and Tom, parents of ten, regularly received bags of clothes just dropped off on their doorstep. What they couldn't use, they gave to us. When we finished with the clothes, we passed them on to others. If you give things directly to friends or acquaintances who need them, there's a much better chance that you will do some good. You can also donate to thrift shops such as the Salvation Army, but sometimes it's best to cut out the middleman and keep charity on a person-to-person level.

Serve Your Community by Your Words

While we serve our neighbors' physical needs, we also have a grace-filled chance to take care of their spiritual needs. Our friend Tony lamented that he hadn't given more and said more to his many "godchildren," sons of single mothers who passed through his life and who had no father figure but him. "I used to talk about a lot of stupid stuff. Now I talk only about God. I used to give only myself, when I could have been giving Christ," he said.

"Often the deepest cause of suffering is the very absence of God," stated Benedict XVI (*Deus Caritas Est* [*DCE*], 31). You can alleviate that suffering by telling people how God is at work in your life and by giving others a reason to hope. When you instruct, advise, console, and comfort those who seek your help, you share Christ with them (*CCC*, 2447). There's no need to preach in the middle of Times Square. There are people all around us who don't know the depths of Christ's love. If someone asks a question about your faith, don't be afraid to answer (see 1 Pt 3:15).

Religion has a unique perspective to offer on virtually every issue that touches our lives. It answers questions about the meaning of life, marriage, family, and community. When you explain with conviction that you believe, love, give, and sacrifice because you want to do God's will, it reveals to people that God can be the source and center of a happy, fulfilled, and meaningful life.

When you value your friendship with God, you want to introduce him to others. When you are in love with God, you glow with joy, peace, and enthusiasm. Christian joy, expressed through ordinary conversation, will make people wonder if Christ could truly be the way, the truth, and the promise of eternity. But our words must come from a place of caring, of relationship. If we don't open our hearts to people before we open our mouths, we will be "a noisy gong or a clanging symbol" (1 Cor 13:1). Tell truth to people because you want to help them, not because you want to win an argument or be acknowledged as right.

Our belief in the truth should spark a passionate desire to receive and reflect God's caring and mercy to all. "If love needs truth, truth also needs love. Love and truth are inseparable. Without love, truth becomes cold, impersonal and oppressive for people's day-to-day lives."[1] Caring merges with truth to craft a compassionate solution.

Serve Your Parish

Every parish community provides ample opportunities to serve your neighbors. In fact, one purpose of a parish is to "[practice] the charity of the Lord in good works and brotherly love" (CCC, 2179). As members of Christ's body, we are meant to be broken and shared with our brothers and sisters (see 1 Cor 11:24 and Rom 12:5). Unmet needs are all around us, sometimes hidden where we would least expect it.

The religious education teachers at our suburban middle-class parish tell stories about children who struggle with deep unanswered questions about God. In the confidential diaries they write for Confirmation preparation, the children reveal their confusion and depression, the rampant sex and drug and alcohol use that surround them, and their doubt that a good God even exists. In most cases, it seems the parents have no idea what their teenage children are going through. Elementary school-children tell their catechists that they want to go to Mass on Sundays, but their parents won't take them. Volunteering to be a catechist is truly volunteering for the missions in our midst.

Even church music can be a powerful ministry. Our former choir, Musica pro Domino, used to travel to parishes all around the tri-state area. Inspired by John Paul II's *Letter to Artists,* our choir conductor made it her mission to bring back into the liturgy centuries of the world's greatest Catholic music, including Gregorian chant and the exquisite soaring sound of unaccompanied polyphony.

Most people in our choir had no musical or vocal training and couldn't even read music when they joined. But they were in love with God and were passionate about sharing their music. Once after the choir sang for a Mass in New Jersey, an elderly parishioner walked up to us and said, "Thank you so much. I felt like this was the first time I really attended Mass in the last forty years." By sharing beauty, you can bring people closer to God.

One of our favorite ways to share our faith is through pre-Cana classes, working with engaged couples. A close friend admitted she had learned only the bare rudiments of Catholicism when she was a girl, and she was looking to pre-Cana to make up the lack. In fact, preparation for the Sacrament of Matrimony is often the only religious education routinely attended by adults. It's often the first religious education they've attended since they were teenagers preparing for the Sacrament of Confirmation. If you know your faith and love your married life, volunteer for pre-Cana and you will help so many!

People close to you are yearning to know what's so good about Catholicism, what's so wonderful about faith, and what's so awesome about God. By feeding someone's faith, you will serve a need that is soul deep.

Go to the Outskirts

Pope Francis constantly encourages Catholics to step outside their comfort zones, to be missionaries, to go to the outskirts among people who suffer in material or spiritual poverty. "The Lord asks us . . . to make ourselves the neighbor of those farthest away" (*CCC*, 1825). When we serve people within our geographical or parish communities, we are without a doubt loving our neighbor. But the Church has a soft spot, a "preferential love," for the poorest of the poor (*CCC*, 2448).

Especially in major urban areas, the poorest of the poor are often right in front of us—or within a short drive. Our friends Connie and Tom, parents of ten, routinely drive from Long Island into New York City at wintertime to give old coats, warm clothes, and bags of burgers from the fast-food dollar menu to the first homeless people they see. Our friend Nirveen, although disabled because of blindness, regularly organizes dozens of people to distribute sandwiches to the homeless men and women sleeping overnight in New York City's Penn Station.

Traveling recently with our ten-year-old daughter, Maria, to New York City, we saw numerous people begging for money, some on subway cars and others on the subway platforms. Maria couldn't understand why most passengers refused even to look at the people who asked them for money. People stared at their feet or rushed by without pausing, not placing any money in the rattling cups of coins.

We explained to Maria that, after seeing dozens of pleading requests every day, ordinary people just give up thinking they could ever meet the constant need of so many. And, of course, it's good to exercise conscientious charity, investigating when we can how our money will be used. But Maria insisted on giving money to everyone who asked. So we fought our way back against the stream of foot traffic to drop money in the cup of a man we had just passed by. Because of a little girl's example, this former urbanite felt and acted a little less jaded!

Of course, the poorest of the poor don't live only in urban areas. In the rural area where I grew up, many farming families living outside town lines lack access to basic municipal services such as garbage removal and water supply. Small-town dwellers like my parents make it a point to help out lower-income folks in the surrounding countryside. While visiting my parents in Virginia, Manny has often joined Opa in building houses for the rural poor through the charitable organization Habitat for Humanity. You don't need to look hard or go far to find ways to help the poorest of the poor.

In the end, we face higher accountability for disregarding the needy that God places in our path. In the parable of the rich man and the beggar at his gate, Jesus explained how the rich man ignored the beggar at his very doorstep, never giving him a scrap from the table. At the end of their lives, the rich man went to hell while the poor man went to heaven (see Lk 16:19–24). The poor are always with us, and we cannot help them all. But we can at least help the ones whose need is staring us in the face.

The Gospel of Life

Jesus' saving mission, which we share, encompassed not only relieving the physical distress of the poor but also proclaiming the good news to them (see Lk 4:18). Because of this our parish's Respect Life Committee is equally committed to providing for both the spiritual and physical needs of the impoverished women they serve. The committee collects monetary donations for the local

residences that house single pregnant women in need
of support. It also holds a baby shower asking for baby
clothes, baby bottles, blankets, and diapers for the babies
once they're born.

To witness to the dignity of life in a visible way, our
parish Respect Life Committee members venture into the
lower-income town next door to join the Forty Days for
Life prayer campaign. During this annual nationwide
event, volunteers commit to peaceful prayer of the Rosary
outside a local abortion clinic every day during Respect
Life month in the fall and Lent in the spring.

On the designated mornings, standing in front of an
abortion facility on an unfamiliar street in an unfamiliar
town (our town has no abortion clinic), a small band of
us gather to recite the Rosary and to offer information
about services for expectant mothers. Initially, we were
afraid. But the more frequently we traveled there, the
less nervous we became. One day a large group of locals
approached us. We held our ground, wondering what
they would have to say. "You're doing a good thing," they
said. "Join us next time!" we invited.

Acts of charity can create common cause between
people we don't normally consider to be our neighbors.
As the parable of the Good Samaritan teaches, everyone
is our neighbor. In this well-beloved parable, a man was
attacked by robbers and left for dead by the side of the
road. Ignored by the priest and the Levite (also a member
of Israel's priestly class), only the hated outsider—the
Samaritan—rescued the stranger in need, bandaging his
wounds, bringing him to an inn, and paying for the inn-
keeper to tend to him. Only the Good Samaritan acted
like a true neighbor (see Lk 10:25–37).

What's more, the Good Samaritan gave the poor victim a very personal and intimate kind of care. The details
of the parable reveal that the Good Samaritan poured oil

and wine on the sufferer's wounds, bandaged him with his own hands, placed him on his own mount, and tended to him at the inn until the Samaritan needed to continue his journey. The Good Samaritan was "personally present" in his gift of charity in the way Benedict XVI insisted all of us must be (*DCE*, 34).

You, too, can be personally present in your acts of charity. A smile, a touch on the shoulder, or a direct gaze into the other person's eyes acknowledges your common humanity and your solidarity. You can also give of your personal time. My brother, Harrison, wouldn't just give money to a hungry man on the street; he would sit down and eat with him at a table at the nearest pizza parlor. Treating the person we are helping as equal to us in dignity is essential in order for our charity "not to prove a source of humiliation" (*DCE*, 34). It is essential in truly serving our neighbor.

We all have a deep-seated need, placed within us by God, to leave the world better off than when we found it. Through acts of charity, we accomplish that goal one person at a time. We can live as if the love of God and the love of neighbor are one inseparable commandment, with the love of our God whom we can't see inspiring us to love the neighbor whom we can see. In the words of Pope Benedict XVI, "Those who draw near to God do not withdraw from men, but rather become truly close to them" (*DCE*, 42). Impelled by gratitude for everything we've been given, we can joyfully serve others by our deeds, words, and love.

Bonus Material

Conversation Starters

- How often do you practice the virtue of hospitality by inviting people into your home?

- What cause motivates you the most, and how would you like to get involved?
- Is there a cause that motivates you both equally?
- What are some service projects you might take up as a family to meet the physical and spiritual needs of your neighbors?

Action Plan

Think about how you can best serve your neighbor while balancing your obligations to your family. Start small with a one-time event, whether it's picking up an extra gallon of milk at the store or donating food to your local church or food pantry. Involve your spouse and children, if you can.

Catechism Corner

"Love for the poor . . . extends not only to material poverty but also to the many forms of cultural and religious poverty" (CCC, 2444).

PART III

CALLED TO BE FRUITFUL

Physical and Spiritual Fertility as Signs of God's Infinite Love

The third key to everlasting married love is fruitfulness. In the beginning of time, "God blessed man and woman with the words: 'Be fruitful and multiply'" (*CCC*, 1652 quoting Gn 1:28). Our sexuality and our fertility are great gifts from our Creator, and the children who are produced or welcomed into the circle of your love are the crown of your marriage.

Modernity isn't sure whether children are a blessing or a burden. They were always considered a great sign of God's favor in the Old Testament. In a quintessentially Mediterranean image of richness and abundance, the Psalms rejoice that "your wife will be like a fruitful vine within your house; your children will be like olive shoots around your table" (128:3).

Today's reality is more complicated. In a nonagricultural society, children are sometimes thought of more as a burden than a blessing. Fertility can feel like a cross, but infertility can feel like one, too. Through advocating methods of Natural Family Planning, the Church proposes solutions for those struggling with fertility and infertility alike. And through insisting that children with special needs are blessings, too, the Church extends her loving arms around parents who have welcomed special-needs children into their families.

Of course, fertility is more than just biological. It has a spiritual component as well. When Jesus said in John 15:5 that those who live in him will "bear much fruit," he was referring to a harvest of souls, good works, and eternal reward. A married couple's love for one another cannot remain closed in on itself. It is meant to be generously shared with others—whether biological children, adopted children, foster children, stepchildren, or even anyone seeking friendship and spiritual advice. Every person we counsel, encourage, or inspire by our visible dedication to the other brings us one step closer to a better world (CCC, 1653, 2379).

7.

Turning Spouses into Life-Giving Lovers

THE CREATIVE POWER OF SEX

> At the moment of conjugal union . . . a man and woman, in the "truth" of their masculinity and femininity, become a mutual gift to each other.
> —Pope John Paul II, *Letter to Families*, 12

Manny and I had yet another one of our bombshell conversations while we sat in downtown Tokyo in our favorite Italian restaurant. Although I had left for Japan a few short months after we met, he had flown across the ocean to spend Valentine's Day with me. I was hoping for a marriage proposal, but he felt we still had more to discuss. As we debated whether using chopsticks on spaghetti was really a good idea, Manny raised the subject of virginity.

"I'm not a virgin," he admitted, "and I'm sorry about that. My virginity is something I wish I could give to the woman I marry. But it's not something I can give to you."

My mind reeled in shock, not because of his admission but because of how important he thought virginity was. It didn't fit the story line of the romance novels I read, in which the hero makes a gift of his years (and years and years) of sexual experience with dozens of swooningly satisfied women.

Once again, Manny had blindsided me with his radically different point of view. *How could anyone still see virginity as a gift?* I wondered. Of course, as anyone with a passing acquaintance of John Paul II's theology of the body knows, our virginity, our sexuality, and our very bodies are great gifts. And when we have sex with another person, we are not just sharing our body; we are sharing our entire self.

Catholicism doesn't encourage saving sex for marriage because it characterizes sex as dirty or bad. It encourages saving sex for marriage because it is such a precious gift, worthy of being shared only in the nurturing, protected, and lifelong bond of marriage. The *Catechism* states that sexuality is not merely biological. Rather, it "is a source of joy and pleasure" that, between married people, is also "a sign and pledge of spiritual communion" (CCC, 2360, 2361, 2362). In other words, sex isn't just good; it's sacred. But it is good only in its proper context. That context is marriage.

Healthy notions of sex can make a good marriage very good, but unhealthy notions of sex can burden a marriage for years. Every premarital sexual encounter we have leaves behind memories, expectations, points of comparison, and often regrets and deep heartbreak. In walking away from a past sexual relationship, we often walk away from a part of ourselves, a part that we've shared and can't get back. Sex within marriage can allow us to heal mistaken ideas about the worth of sexuality and about our own self-worth.

There are two common misconceptions about sex that can interfere with having a good marriage. The first misconception is that sex should be used only for procreation and that any pleasure we get from sex is a necessary evil. This attitude is sometimes called Puritanical, Victorian, or Manichean. But by any name it is mistaken because it ignores the *unitive* purpose of sex (*LR*, 43–45).

The second misconception about sex is that its primary purpose is physical pleasure and that the creation of new life is an unnecessary and troublesome side effect. This ignores the true drama and power of sex. It changes sex from something that is open, vulnerable, and courageous to something that is just fun—such as shopping or watching the game on TV (*LR*, 46–48). This attitude unfairly downplays the *procreative* purpose of sex.

In Search of Everlasting Love

How Can Sex within Marriage Have the
Power to Heal Hearts and Minds?

Larry, a twenty-six-year-old man with a porn addiction, was drawn to thirty-five-year-old Conchita because she seemed so pure and innocent. Larry had started viewing porn as a teenager and regularly masturbated while viewing porn at least two or three times a week. Although he mentioned his habit to Conchita, he downplayed it significantly before they were married. Despite Larry's addiction, he had very little sexual experience with women. Conchita was a virgin.

The wedding night was very painful for Conchita, and sexual relations between them progressively got worse and worse. Burdened with an overly strict religious upbringing,

Conchita expected sex to be gross and uncomfortable, a necessary evil. She did not like her husband to see her naked, although she was happy to be touched. Larry was unused to foreplay, which added to Conchita's discomfort. Torn between pleasure and guilt, he felt like a dirty husband trying to force sex on his wife. Neither Larry nor Conchita believed that sex could be a beautifully intimate act.

A few months after their wedding, Conchita caught Larry looking at porn, which devastated her and shamed him, creating a wall between them. In therapy, they were advised to read John Paul II's book *Love and Responsibility*, which explains the essential goodness of the sexual relationship between husband and wife. Reading the book helped to identify and correct errors that each of them had in their view of sexuality, and it helped open up avenues of discussion between them. Larry was referred to Sexaholics Anonymous for help in overcoming his porn addiction. He was also advised to touch his wife often in a nonsexual manner, holding her hands or rubbing her shoulders, so they could grow accustomed to feeling pleasure in each other's touch.

Reflection Questions

1. How did Conchita and Larry's pasts affect their views of sexuality?
2. Why was John Paul II's book so helpful for them?
3. How did sex in their marriage begin to heal their misconceptions?

Manny's Diagnosis

Conchita's upbringing communicated the overly simplistic view that all sex was bad. Larry's habit of porn and masturbation had given him the mistaken idea that marriage was all about his own on-demand sexual satisfaction. Through ongoing therapy, Conchita and Larry were able to embrace a healthier, wholesome, and more loving understanding of sexuality. In resolving her marital problems, Conchita changed longstanding misconceptions about herself and her body. Meanwhile, Larry learned the importance of self-control and putting his partner and her needs first.

Sex is not a necessary evil or a dirty act of self-gratification. It is a gift from a loving God, a gift that brings pleasure, happiness, togetherness, and the power to create new life (CCC, 2366). It is a physical intimacy that opens the door to greater emotional and spiritual intimacy.

Becoming One Flesh

Sex unites a couple when they give to one another everything that they are, no holding back. This total gift of self can occur only within marriage, when two people have pledged to unite their whole selves, souls and bodies, as long as they both shall live (CCC, 1643–1644). Without the full commitment of marriage, sex might bring physical satisfaction but leave the heart and soul untouched and unfulfilled.

Research surveys confirm the benefits of married sex: "Married people have both more and better sex than singles do. They not only have sex more often, but they enjoy it more, both physically and emotionally, than do their unmarried counterparts. Only cohabiters have more sex than married couples, but they don't necessarily enjoy it as much."[1]

Why is married sex better? Perhaps the spouses have the freedom to surrender themselves totally to one another, without fear. This doesn't mean the level of physical enjoyment necessarily stays at a constant high. Sexual desire fluctuates according to people's age, stress level, physical health, and whether they're experiencing underlying problems in the marital relationship. But in a lifelong relationship, couples can take a long-term view. They can be patient with themselves and with their spouses, and be as content to give as to receive—to give comfort, pleasure, reassurance, affirmation, and love.

John Paul II explained that our deepest yearnings as human beings are met when we make "a sincere gift of self" to another. "All married life is a gift," he said, but husbands and wives feel this most strongly when they reach out to touch each other in love and "bring about that encounter which makes them 'one flesh' (Gn 2:24)" (*LF*, 12). The love in their hearts and the sacramental union of their souls become tangible through their bodies.

While it is true that some newlyweds approach sex with a natural joy and spontaneity—without hang-ups, body-image issues, or ego problems, and able to learn each other's needs and preferences in the privacy of the marriage bed—it isn't that simple for everyone. One newlywed blogger told us that many twentysomethings have a great theoretical understanding of the Catholic view of sexuality because of the popularity of programs based on John Paul II's theology of the body. But they don't understand how it works in practice.

What is a healthy sex life, and how do you develop it after marriage? A healthy married sex life combines physical, emotional, and spiritual intimacy.

Physical intimacy involves exploring and responding to each other's bodies using all five senses. Candlelight, moonlight, and daylight each add their own ambience.

Gregorian chant, rock and roll, salsa, or Wagner's "Ride of the Valkyries" can enhance the mood of the moment, whatever it is! Scented candles, incense, or perfume can create a romantic atmosphere. And of course there are your senses of taste and touch. Holy sex doesn't have to be dull!

Emotionally healthy sex is about letting the other person "in" to the most private space in your heart and about meeting the other person's needs and desires as well as communicating your own. Sexual pleasure isn't meant to be taken as a right or withheld as a power play; it's meant to be shared. For this reason, in the sexology chapter of his book *Love and Responsibility*, John Paul II recommended that spouses strive to achieve simultaneous orgasms (257–258). Even in its most intimate details, sex is about a *mutual* sharing of self, always serving the other for the good of both.

We'll take a look at the characteristics of spiritually healthy sex in the next section. First, let's consider the following case study that addresses an issue that is common among couples whose inexperience (or bad experiences) with sex make it difficult to enter fully into intimacy.

In Search of Everlasting Love

How Can Couples Get Comfortable Talking about Sex?

Matt and Rachel were both virgins on their wedding night and were nervous about the sexual aspect of their marriage. Soon after the wedding, they realized that Matt had problems with premature ejaculation. They were advised to stop having sex for a while and to concentrate only on foreplay.

Unfortunately, Rachel objected to having her breasts or genitals touched during foreplay, although she denied any history of sexual abuse. In therapy, Matt and Rachel were asked to draw a picture of their bodies, label the areas where they did and didn't enjoy being touched, and assign a rating of one to ten, with one being the least enjoyable and ten being the most enjoyable. Matt gave the highest ratings to his lips and genitals. Rachel gave the highest ratings to her lips and ears but the lowest ratings to her breasts and genitals.

To help Matt with his premature ejaculation problem, the two of them were advised to concentrate on foreplay and learning each other's bodies without worrying about completing the sexual act. To help Rachel relax, Matt was advised to start by stimulating her lips and ears and move slowly toward her more sensitive areas. Matt and Rachel were both very happy with the results.

Reflection Questions

1. Why was it helpful for Rachel and Matt to label a diagram rather than discussing their sex life more directly?
2. Why was Rachel so uncomfortable being touched?
3. What did the couple learn about their different rates of arousal?

Manny's Diagnosis

In Matt and Rachel's chaste courtship, they avoided speaking about sexuality because they considered it inappropriate. They were also not in the habit of joking or talking about sexuality with their friends and family. Labeling a diagram allowed them to be explicit without actually saying things in a way that still felt inappropriate. Rachel was uncomfortable being touched out of nervousness and unfamiliarity with such powerful new sensations. The couple learned that Matt needed to take his time with Rachel so they could both be happy.

Try something similar to what Matt and Rachel did, and tell each other your five most favorite and least favorite spots to be touched (or use a diagram if you prefer). That's a great way to start a conversation about sexuality.

Building Healthy Body Image

One of the greatest gifts of married life is appreciating the beauty of our own bodies by learning to accept our spouse's assessment of our attributes. Some women struggle with a negative body image and criticize themselves harshly for their perceived flaws—a flabby belly, wide hips, skinny legs, small breasts, or big hands—you name it; there's a chance some woman somewhere will feel bad about it. And yet men are often far more forgiving of "flaws" in their wives' naked bodies.

When I become too self-critical, Manny objects: "Hey! That's my wife you're talking about!" A wife who sees herself through her husband's eyes can learn to be more accepting of her own body. And her renewed self-confidence will make her even more attractive to her husband.

Whereas women can be overly conscious of body-image issues, men can easily be wounded if they sense their wives are not sexually satisfied. Communicating what feels good and what doesn't is an essential part of developing physical and emotional intimacy. In turn, deeper emotional intimacy gives the couple even greater freedom to express their needs without inhibition. It doesn't have to be perfect every time. Learning how to make one another happy in bed, like learning how to make one another happy out of bed, is a work in progress. Positive, encouraging, gentle, and compassionate communication is the key to achieving physical, emotional, and spiritual intimacy.

The Quest for Spiritual Intimacy

As with physical and emotional intimacy, spiritual intimacy is something that develops with time. Remember to thank God for the closeness the two of you experience in your marriage. Cuddling in bed at night to share highlights of your day and maybe praying a decade of the Rosary can be a fabulous segue into making love. One couple we know kneels down together and recites the prayer of Tobias and Sarah: "We take each other 'not because of lust, but with sincerity' and love" (Tb 8:7). Anyone who has ever struggled to relinquish the lingering guilt or baggage of past relationships might find this prayer helpful (along with going to the Sacrament of Reconciliation).

Spiritual intimacy in the bedroom can have a healing effect on the rest of your life as well. When lovemaking becomes an expression of trust and faith in God's will for the future, it can bind the spouses together when it feels as if other things in the marriage are falling apart. America's most famous convert couple, Scott and Kimberly Hahn, tell a beautiful story about how their commitment to make love regularly helped them through a very difficult time in their marriage.

Scott, who was an evangelical Protestant minister, converted to Catholicism, but his wife, Kimberly, wanted to remain Protestant. Kimberly explained that she and her husband "needed some tangible expression of our unity in the midst of our disunity. . . . If we were furious with each other, not feeling like the other had listened, we had to resolve things enough to be able to express love genuinely and physically."[2]

Of course, making love did not entirely solve their problem, which was ultimately resolved only when they were both confirmed in the Catholic faith. Yet sex gave them the grace and strength to make it through the long, rocky, and painful period when speaking about their problems was unbearably difficult and Kimberly even considered leaving her husband. As Kimberly said, "God used the act of marriage, open to life, to carry us through conflict that could have ended badly."[3]

Overcoming the Past

Growing numbers of young Catholics today are defying the pressure of popular culture and are living their single lives as virgin, chaste, and proud. We hold immense admiration for these people. Sadly, Manny and I did not have their strength. Although our own courtship was chaste, we both had pasts. We were open and honest with each other from the beginning of our relationship. We fought almost Herculean battles to forgive ourselves and each other, frequently resorting to the confessional. We wanted to turn over a new leaf. We wanted a different relationship, a pure relationship, a relationship that could last.

"How far is too far?" was a big question in our dating relationship, just as it is for many couples. Manny finally decided that all we could do was hold hands. When he told me his decision, I felt he'd kicked me in the gut. To me, my sexiness was my self-worth. If this man didn't want me (or wasn't willing to use me) as a sexual being, then in my own eyes I had no value. But by controlling his passion for me before we were married, Manny was showing me that he valued all of me and was assuring me of his ability to stay faithful to me after marriage. In order to reach this realization, I had to reject nearly every attitude on sex I had absorbed from the culture around me.

Today's culture places such a high value on sexiness that it's easy to see ourselves as sex objects, rated on a scale of one to ten. But we are whole persons, complex and multitalented, with so much more to give. Romance novels and TV shows frequently equate "best sex you'll ever have" with "best spouse you'll ever have" as if marriage could be reduced to the marriage bed or as if worth as a marital partner could be assessed only between the sheets.

Premarital relationships often reinforce the primacy of sex, since couples may share sex and fun and little else. Sex becomes a habit, switching sexual partners becomes routine, and marriage seems like the latest in a string of sexual encounters, distinguished only by the extravagance of the wedding day.

Although often characterized as harmless or even normal, pornography is especially damaging to a relationship, as it diminishes both the dignity of the human person and God's design for our sexuality. The *Catechism* states that pornography constitutes "a grave offense." Porn "offends against chastity because it perverts the conjugal act. . . . It immerses all who are involved in the illusion of a fantasy world" (*CCC*, 2354). Often developed in the teenage or even preteen years, the habit of viewing pornography can create a warped view of sexual relationships before they even start.

In the opinion of Dr. Richard Fitzgibbons, addiction to Internet porn—a type of compulsive sexual behavior—is devastating more Catholic marriages and families today than any other addictive behavior. Porn use increases dissatisfaction and loneliness in the marriage. It weakens trust and spiritual vitality, it lessens the addicted person's desire for his or her spouse, and it leads more easily to adultery. In his 2006 pastoral letter, Bishop Paul Loverde stated, "This plague stalks the souls of men, women and children, ravages the bonds of marriage and victimizes the most innocent among us. It obscures and destroys people's ability to see one another as unique and beautiful expressions of God's creation, instead darkening their vision, causing them to view others as objects to be used and manipulated."[4]

Out of all the problems from a person's past, an addiction to Internet porn is the most likely to require assistance from a mental health professional.

Overcoming Infidelity

Unsolved issues from the past can create dangerous fault lines in a marriage. For women in particular, having a higher number of premarital sexual partners is linked to less happiness in marriage.[5] A pattern of multiple sexual partners before marriage can also make it easier to give in to the temptation of sexual infidelity afterward. An extramarital affair can destroy in a heartbeat the physical, emotional, and spiritual intimacy that spouses have worked to develop for years.

In Search of Everlasting Love

What Are the Warning Signs of Future Infidelity?

Ben habitually flirted with women at work. He considered it harmless. When he attended a summer party with his wife, Madeleine, he admired how the other female guests looked in their bikinis in the hot tub. Then he surprised himself by actually kissing one of them.

He didn't consider it important enough to tell Madeleine.

One day, Ben was casually looking at his wife's computer and noticed that her e-mail program was open. Curious, he began reading and found ongoing conversations between Madeleine and one of her ex-boyfriends. He confronted her, and she insisted that the conversations amounted to a bit of harmless flirting, even though the ex-boyfriend was urging her to meet up in person.

Realizing how wounded he was by Madeleine's e-mail exchange made Ben take stock and consider how his own actions might be hurting his wife and how flirting could lead the way to more serious infidelity.

Reflection Questions

1. Is flirting such as Ben's harmless or not?
2. Should Ben have told Madeleine that he kissed another woman?
3. Was Madeleine's email conversation with her ex-boyfriend a problem?

Manny's Diagnosis

Although many people consider flirting to be harmless, it sends the signal that the person is attracted and open to a romantic dalliance. It blurs the line between an appropriate and an inappropriate relationship. When a spouse steps over the line and shares with someone else the kind of physical affection that rightly belongs only to his or her spouse, the spouse may consider hiding it in order not to damage the marital relationship. But deception and lying often pave the way to a full-blown affair. Affairs can also start through emotional intimacy, like sharing inner thoughts and feelings with someone other than your mate. Emotional intimacy like Madeleine's frequent e-mail contact with her ex-boyfriend can also lead to physical infidelity. Similarly, social media can make it extremely easy and perhaps tempting to contact people from your past, including past romances.

The first rule for avoiding infidelity is to avoid temptation. The Bible story of King David's adultery with Bathsheba provides a basic road map (2 Sm 11). First, King David saw Bathsheba bathing, and he didn't look away from her beauty. Then he ordered Bathsheba brought to the palace so he could meet her in person. Soon after, he began an affair with her. Ultimately, the king used his power to deceive and destroy, sending Uriah, Bathsheba's husband, to die on the battlefield so the king could keep her for himself. Each compromising choice led King David closer to the final destructive ending. The best thing he could have done at the beginning was simply to look away.

Infidelity comes in many forms, some more serious than others—ongoing affairs, serial one-night stands, visiting strip clubs, heavy porn use or addiction, explicitly sexual romance novels or TV shows, fantasizing about someone other than your spouse, and even confiding in or keeping secrets with anyone who isn't your spouse or confessor. Any of these things has the potential to weaken or destroy the marriage bond.

The good news is that even outright infidelity doesn't have to be a death knell for a marriage if both spouses

commit to working through it by taking four immediate
positive steps to rebuild or HEAL the marriage:

1. Honestly confront the issues that led to the infidelity
    (as well as any future backsliding).

2. Eliminate the infidelity, making a clean break with
    the offending relationship.

3. Be Accountable to a disinterested party, establishing a
    relationship with a priest, therapist, or spiritual direc-
    tor to prevent relapse.

4. Limit temptation. In addition to breaking off the inap-
    propriate relationship, avoid unnecessary contact
    with people and places that encouraged the infidelity
    to start with.

This kind of reconciliation is a powerful example
of self-giving love, in which the betrayed spouse works
through feelings of grief, anger, and self-doubt for the
good that is still in the marriage, especially if there are
children. Betrayed spouses will face their own set of
temptations, such as punishing the offending spouse or
using the knowledge of the affair as ammunition in unre-
lated arguments.

An important step in reconciling is for both spouses
to examine their patterns of speech and behavior and listen for any problems in the marriage that might have led
the offending spouse to seek out the affair as an escape.
In many cases, the couple will need professional help to
identify and resolve these underlying problems. Rebuild-
ing trust might take years, but it can eventually happen
with continuous caring and patience on both sides.

The Creative Power of Physical Fertility

Although sex affects us strongly on the deepest emotional level, the truly awesome power of sex is revealed in its fertility, particularly its amazing capacity to generate new life. As our friend Donna tells her teenage students, "Of course sex is powerful. It makes babies!"

Through the conception of a child, a husband and wife are bound together closer than ever before. They become one flesh, even on a biological level. The DNA of the father and the mother combine in a new human being. And the Holy Spirit is there, too, contributing the new person's soul. It is difficult to imagine a closer unity among husband, wife, and God.

Parents share in God's creative power by conceiving and giving birth to a member of the next generation. We become cocreators, entering into the cosmic current of existence (*LR*, 38). Since we are cocreators with God, then like him, we can appreciate each child for its own sake and not for the sake of what the child can do for us (*LF*, 9–10). Having a child is not a way of fulfilling ourselves. It is a way of fulfilling God's plans for us. This trust in God's plans for our fertility lies at the heart of the Catholic marriage ceremony, when the priest asks the couple, "Will you accept children lovingly from God?" (*LF*, 16).

Each of our children is God's gift to us. "The newborn child gives itself to its parents by the very fact of its coming into existence" (*LF*, 11), and the mere existence of a child entitles it to our love. Our love for our children should not depend on how cute, talented, good-natured, or healthy they are. God's love for us is not conditioned on those things. He loves us for ourselves alone, and we ought to pass that unconditional love on to our children (*LF*, 9).

God loves each child from its very conception. "Before I formed you in the womb I knew you," the Lord tells us in Jeremiah 1:5. Moreover, the birth of each new child reflects Christ's resurrection and his victory over death (*LF*, 11).

This message struck home in a compelling way at my grandfather's funeral. My brother had just had his first child, a little girl named Andi Dakota, and she attended the funeral service with the rest of the family. As babies do, she cried and gurgled occasionally throughout the service.

We thought that the baby noises might have disturbed some of the people at the funeral. But more than one person walked up to the family and said how nice it was to hear a baby at a funeral. It reminded them that life continues even after death and that my grandfather's legacy would continue through his great-grandchildren. As Psalm 128:6 states in the words of a beautiful blessing, "May you see your children's children," or in this case, your grandchildren's children.

The Grace of Emotional Fertility

Just as sexuality has physical, emotional, and spiritual components, so does fertility. Sexual fidelity in marriage, a commitment to a lifelong and exclusive bond, generates a deep sense of emotional stability and security. No one else can touch or be touched by your spouse the way you can. You have a physical relationship like no other and an emotional relationship like no other as well. This emotional bond can bear great fruit.

Deep in the soul, people feel an intense yearning to seek the good and to rejoice when they have found it. This natural yearning is intensified and perfected by grace. Through the sacramental graces of matrimony, married people can seek after the good more passionately, find it more successfully, and delight in it more joyfully. Even better, they can help their spouse to do the same!

A husband is his wife's strongest supporter. A wife is her husband's biggest fan. "You always have to stand in your spouse's corner," said a friend from social media, "because most of the world won't." The world is difficult enough, and good spouses build each other up, not tear each other down.

Our friend Kurt credits his wife, Bianca, with completely turning his life around. He was a college dropout working a dead-end job because he couldn't afford the tuition to finish his degree. But Bianca believed in him and in his dream to go to law school. She took over the family finances and rehabilitated his credit. Through her encouragement, Kurt entered a third-tier law school and then transferred to a better one. Bianca never let him give up, constantly reassuring him that he had what it took to succeed. He now works for a nationally known law firm. "With my brawn (hard work, willingness to be the sole breadwinner) and her brains (believing in me and having big plans for us), we were able to do what neither of us could do alone," Kurt said.

Bearing Spiritual Fruit

The full significance of fertility in marriage "can be understood only in reference to *man's eternal destiny*," according to the *Catechism* (*CCC*, 2371). In other words, spouses are called to be mothers and fathers in a spiritual sense—they are called to be supernaturally fruitful. In a very beautiful passage often reprinted in parish bulletins on Mother's Day, Joseph Cardinal Mindszenty spoke about the spiritual dimensions of motherhood: "The angels have not been blessed with such a grace. They cannot share in God's creative miracle to bring new saints to Heaven. Only a human mother can."[6]

The presence of a father also plays a crucial role in his children's spiritual well-being. In the play *The Radiation of Fatherhood*, authored before he was elected Pope John Paul II, Fr. Karol Wojtyla suggested that the human father's task is to imitate or "radiate" the fatherhood of God. Modern psychotherapists also theorize that the way people relate to their father mirrors the way they relate to God. Through parenting as lovingly as they can, fathers have a chance to teach their children to see God as the loving Father that he is.

A biological link is not necessary to be supernatural parents. Priests, consecrated religious, and married couples without children can all lead lives of spiritual fruitfulness. We are spiritually fruitful whenever we nurture others (see *CCC*, 2379). We know a married couple who chose to live with the poor in a Catholic Worker house of hospitality for the homeless, because this couple could not have biological children and they wanted to give more of themselves to the Church and the world. These spouses serve their vocation to marriage by providing physical and spiritual help to others and by guiding and tending their souls.

Fruitfulness Is a Blessing

In this modern industrial or postindustrial world, fertility is not always seen as a good thing. Children require the expenditure of money, time, and effort while offering few tangible benefits in return, particularly in the early years. Focusing too much on the financial burden of child rearing can almost lead couples to fear having children. "Life is often perceived not as a blessing, but as a danger from which to defend oneself" (*FC*, 6).

In addition, many parents and sex educators try to discourage teenage sex by emphasizing the downsides of pregnancy. "You'll never graduate high school," "Your career chances will be ruined," or even, "Get pregnant, and I'll throw you out of this house!" If fear of pregnancy becomes ingrained early on, it's hard to switch mind-sets after marriage and see pregnancy as a good thing.

Plus, the possibility of contraception confronts spouses with the tyranny of choice. Instead of treating marriage itself as the right time to get pregnant, we feel we have to pick the absolutely ideal time to have a child, factoring in dual career goals, financial goals, or life goals. And of course no time is absolutely ideal, if what that means is involving no personal sacrifice. Rather than marriage ending any fear of pregnancy, it can generate a new set of fears of disappointing our own expectations or our spouse's (*LR*, 261–262, 265).

But trusting in God's providence can take away those fears—fears that can seem strongest in people with the best careers, the most money, and the biggest houses. The prospect of becoming a parent can be quite daunting. But when God asks us to be parents, we have the choice to say yes, as did Jesus' mother, Mary. We can stand for life just as the Church stands for life, because "in each human life she sees the splendor of that 'Yes,' that 'Amen,' who is Christ Himself" (*FC*, 30).

Bonus Material
Conversation Starters

- What preconceived notions of sex did you learn from your parents or your peers? Do they differ from the Catholic view of sexuality?
- How easy is it for you and your spouse to talk about sex? Could you communicate even better?

- Do you feel there is a "best time" in a marriage to start having children?
- Do you and your spouse agree on how many children to have? If not, what keeps you from reaching an agreement?

Action Plan

Consider "renewing your vows" by making love at least once a week, especially to celebrate the Lord's Day on Sunday. If there is an issue related to sex or pregnancy that you aren't ready to talk to your spouse about, bring it to prayer and see if you gain any insights.

Catechism Corner

Sex within marriage is "noble and honorable . . . and enriches the spouses in joy and gratitude" (*CCC*, 2362).

8.

Turning the Fear of Fertility into a Total Gift of Self

FINDING A BETTER ALTERNATIVE TO ARTIFICIAL BIRTH CONTROL AND IVF

The difference, both anthropological and moral, between contraception and recourse to the rhythm of the cycle . . . involves in the final analysis two irreconcilable concepts of the human person and of human sexuality.
—Pope John Paul II, *Familiaris Consortio*, 32

Like many professional women at the beginning of their marriages, I felt ambivalent about whether I wanted to have a child right away. I was torn between wanting to make partner in a law firm and wanting to be a mother.

When I went to the obstetrician's office for some tests about four months after getting married, the doctor reported that my hormone levels showed I could not get pregnant. Immediately, getting pregnant became a top priority! We asked friends to pray for us, I began wearing a necklace with a medal of the Infant Jesus of Prague, and I ardently asked God not to let me be infertile.

On the next doctor's visit, surprise! The pregnancy test was positive. When an ultrasound showed that the baby was totally fine and about two months along, I cried with relief and joy. Most likely, my hormone levels at the previous visit had shown that I couldn't get pregnant because I was already carrying a child. Thank God for the mental anguish we went through upon hearing about my possible infertility! That trial dramatically revealed to us that the ability to conceive a child is a great blessing.

We Are Wonderfully Made

The female reproductive system is intricate and beautifully designed. As it says in scripture, we are wonderfully made (see Ps 139:14). Each aspect of a woman's reproductive system is fashioned to nurture new life and bring it to fruition. Whereas men are pretty much constantly fertile, female fertility waxes and wanes. One husband noted with astonishment that he knew about as much about his wife's reproductive system as about the inner workings of a nuclear reactor.

Natural Family Planning (NFP) helps a woman and her husband to become aware of her fertility. It works with rather than against the female body, relying on self-observation of changes in her cycle. Couples who wish to avoid pregnancy defer sex until the infertile part of the wife's cycle, and couples who wish to achieve pregnancy time their intercourse to occur at a time of high fertility.

Fertility is a sign of reproductive health. In no other area of medicine do doctors attempt to prevent the functioning of a healthy bodily system the way that doctors attempt to suppress fertility. Especially as premarital sex becomes almost a foregone conclusion and the age of marriage continues to rise, women can be put into a state of constantly fighting their fertility, chemically suppressing it when it's at its height and then trying to jump-start it as it diminishes.

Fertility, like sex, is a gift from God. NFP works with the gift of fertility in order to help a couple avoid or achieve pregnancy. In contrast with artificial methods of birth control, NFP does not interfere with a healthily functioning human body or treat fertility as a disease to be eradicated. NFP encourages us to be stewards and ministers of our fertility rather than opponents and manipulators of it.

Whenever NFP-practicing couples have sex, they express the truly intimate nature of their sexuality by entering into sex with nothing between them, literally or figuratively. Even (or perhaps especially) if the husband or wife is afraid of a new pregnancy, sex without contraceptives says, "I trust you and God with my future. No matter what happens we'll be okay because we're committed to together forever." The unitive potential of sex is sky high, and the procreative potential is never entirely eliminated (CCC, 2366).

Many people we know have converted (or reverted) to Catholicism after encountering the Church's deeply affirming teachings on the value of our bodies, our sexuality, and our fertility, which reflects the continuing fruitfulness of God's creation. Not every Catholic has experienced the same life-changing encounter, however.

Data from 2006 to 2010 shows that 75 percent of Catholics with a current sexual partner were using artificial birth control at the time of the survey.[1] This widespread acceptance stands in sharp contrast to the Church's long-term opposition to artificial birth control and sterilization, indicating that many Catholics aren't aware of the problems with artificial techniques and the benefits of natural techniques (*CCC*, 2370; *Evangelium Vitae* [*EV*], 13; *Humamae Vitae* [*HV*], 14).

Medical Dangers of Artificial Birth Control

The Pill, the most common form of artificial birth control used by sexually active Catholics, has numerous medical dangers.[2] Package inserts list an increased risk of blood clots, heart attack, stroke, and clinical depression, and an increase in the frequency of breast cancer. Most disturbing, taking birth control pills causes a higher risk of death in smokers over age thirty-five and even in healthy nonsmokers over forty.

As the popularity of organic foods started rising in the early 2000s, the public became more aware of the dangers of synthetic hormones. They realized they didn't want synthetic hormones in their food, and they didn't want them in their bodies either. Growing numbers of non-Catholics began using NFP for purely secular reasons.[3]

Hormonal contraceptives such as the Pill prevent pregnancy in one of three ways: they can prevent ovulation, thicken the cervical mucus to prevent fertilization, or prevent implantation of an already-fertilized egg. This last option is essentially abortive because conception has already occurred and a new life has begun. This abortifacient effect of some hormonal contraceptives is a grave concern for Catholics who believe in the dignity of every human life from conception to natural death.[4]

In addition to the moral concerns about contraception, there are pragmatic concerns as well. Artificial contraception doesn't always work! Failed contraception accounts for more than half of elective abortions performed in this country. According to the Guttmacher Institute, "Fifty-one percent of women who have abortions had used a contraceptive method in the month they got pregnant, most commonly condoms (27%) or a hormonal method (17%)."[5] John Paul II explained that the Catholic Church's opposition to contraception is related to its opposition to abortion: "Contraception and abortion are often closely connected, as fruits of the same tree. . . . [In many instances], such practices . . . imply a self-centered concept of freedom, which regards procreation as an obstacle to personal fulfillment. The life which could result from a sexual encounter thus becomes an enemy to be avoided at all costs, and abortion becomes the only possible decisive response to failed contraception" (*EV*, 13).

In Search of Everlasting Love

Is There a Link between Artificial Contraception and Abortion?

Jerry and Patty, both cradle Catholics, used contraception while they were dating so Patty wouldn't get pregnant. The contraception failed, and Patty insisted on getting an abortion. Although Jerry believed that abortion was wrong, he went along with her decision, reasoning that it was "her body, her choice."

Jerry and Patty later tied the knot, but the abortion had created a rift between them that never healed. As Jerry grew older, he felt more strongly about his faith and started feeling intense regret for the abortion. He felt guilty for not having protected his unborn child. Meanwhile, Patty harbored subconscious resentment toward Jerry for his initially acquiescing in the abortion.

Sensing the widening emotional distance between them, Jerry reached out to Patty, but the couple could not find a way to bridge the gulf between them. Jerry eventually began an extramarital affair with a close female confidante at work. Despite ten years of marriage and three children, Jerry and Patty could not overcome their difficulties, and they divorced.

Reflection Questions

1. Why did Jerry and Patty have premarital sex and use contraception even though it was contrary to the Catholic faith?

2. How might Jerry have responded differently to Patty's announcement that she was pregnant?

3. How did the abortion lead to later marital difficulties?

Manny's Diagnosis

Jerry and Patty wanted to have premarital sex and so they disregarded the Catholic teaching that reserved sex for marriage. Their main concern was not "getting caught" by an unexpected pregnancy. They failed to consider whether they were ready to make a permanent commitment to each other or to any child that might be produced through their sexual intimacy. And so, when the contraception failed, they felt abortion was their only choice.

In reality, Jerry could have offered to marry Patty and support their child. Instead, they set up a pattern of abandonment in their relationship. Jerry essentially abandoned Patty in her crisis pregnancy, leaving her to make a decision on her own. In turn, Patty abandoned Jerry in his later crisis of faith.

Jerry and Patty's story is a true-life example of the link between contraception and abortion pointed out by John

Paul II. Treating fertility as a threat rather than a gift and viewing a child as more a burden than a blessing all too often lead to abortion. This "solution," however, often creates as many problems as it solves. NFP, with its different mind-set, is associated with a lower rate of elective abortion than is failed contraception.[6]

Why NFP Is a Better Alternative to Artificial Birth Control

Many women experience dissatisfaction with various forms of birth control. Some women try as many as six different types of birth control throughout their reproductive lifetime.[7] We know many Catholics who began their married life using artificial contraception and then switched to NFP with great results. Catholics in their forties might be particularly interested in switching to NFP because of the increased health risks that the Pill poses to women of that age. NFP provides a better alternative because it is scientific, effective, physically and relationally healthy, and approved by the Church.

The science of NFP has come a long way in recent decades. The old-fashioned rhythm method involved little more than counting the days between cycles on the calendar. Modern methods of NFP rely on easily observed physical changes called biomarkers. This gives couples real-time information on when ovulation is approaching and when it has already occurred.

The effectiveness of NFP at preventing unintended pregnancy compares favorably with the effectiveness of artificial birth control, not just at perfect use rates but at typical use rates that account for user error. Many people are surprised to learn that the typical use failure rate is 8 percent for the Pill, 16 percent for a diaphragm, 15 percent for a condom, and 29 percent for spermicides. Typical use failure rates for modern methods of NFP fall well within that range; one study even found a failure rate of less than 1 percent.[8] A lot depends on selecting the NFP method that works most effectively with your body and lifestyle (flip to pages 139–142 for help with this).

NFP poses no health risks, since it does not involve putting any chemicals into the body and cannot function as an abortifacient. In addition, scholars at the University of North Carolina, Chapel Hill, have shown that NFP users have as much sex as other couples—approximately five times a month, which is the same as the worldwide average. Best of all, NFP-practicing couples who've never tried any other contraceptive method have a reported divorce rate of two in one thousand—miles lower than the rest of the population.[9]

Be Not Afraid!

The Church approves of NFP as a way to achieve responsible parenthood (CCC, 2370). Because responsible parenthood is an open and generous concept, the *Catechism* cautions that a couple should have "just reasons" to use NFP to avoid pregnancy (CCC, 2368). "Just reasons" look different for every couple and depend dramatically on personal physical, financial, and emotional circumstances.

Reaching agreement on whether or not to avoid pregnancy can be quite a struggle, but it's an important step in understanding each other's deepest needs and becoming more unified as husband and wife. I had a lot of fears about pregnancy early in our marriage, wondering if my first child would mark the end of my professional life. But Manny promised me that he would do whatever it took, work as many jobs as he needed, to provide for his wife and children. With Manny offering me all that he had, how could I say no?

Manny's Story: The Fertility Switch Should Be "On"

In many respects, Karee and I were on the same page about our future. We wanted to get married as soon as possible, and typically in most Catholic dioceses, this means waiting six months. We both agreed that our wedding would take place at Holy Innocents Church on April 29 (the first Saturday after Easter), since it was there that we sang in the choir and there that our romance blossomed.

"When do you think we'll start having kids?" asked my fiancée, glancing at her engagement ring (which had been on her finger less than eight hours). She had always been prone to planning, and this was a pivotal question.

Though we both took it as a given that children would come (God willing), my response took my fiancée by surprise. "I think," I said, uttering each word carefully, as I tend to do when thinking aloud, "that the fertility switch ought to be 'on.' The default position," I said, continuing the analogy, "is for the switch to be 'on,' not 'off.'"

The priest who provided our marriage preparation (the same priest served as a choir conductor and organist and presided at our wedding) did not include NFP as part of the process. I knew NFP was a morally licit means of having a say in how many children we brought into the world, but beyond that I was ignorant on the subject. After the birth of our first child, my wife and I began teaching a course in pre-Cana at the Church of Our Saviour in New York City, where an integral component of a comprehensive course was a section on NFP. Since we knew less than nothing about the mechanics of NFP, we brought in an expert to teach that class.

Several kids later, we decided it was time to get serious about using what we had learned. This brings me to the difficult part of this discussion. NFP, contrary to what

some may believe, is not "Catholic birth control." I would
be willing to accept "Catholic family planning" as a more
accurate term. The difference, you see, is that there are certain times during the month when you either abstain from
sexual intercourse with your wife or accept the possibility
that she might get pregnant. The only sure way to avoid an
unplanned pregnancy is not to have sex. For some people,
that is extremely difficult if not preposterous. So, in a nut-
shell, NFP (used as a method of family planning) consists in
agreeing to abstain from sex with your spouse during certain times of the month (no matter how much you want it).

There are surprising benefits to this. Each month I am
reminded of the longing I experienced years ago when I first
met my wife but did not yet know her in the biblical sense.
Instead of sex we turn toward verbal expressions of love,
prose or poetry, deeds of kindness, or innocent physical
expressions of affection (e.g., holding hands, kissing, or
an occasional foot massage). I know the "green light" will
come eventually, but until then I am once again in "court-
ing mode." In longing for her, I fall in love all over again.
We become playful and flirtatious, and invent ever more
unique euphemisms for the marital act (assuming, perhaps
incorrectly, that our kids will have no idea what we're talking
about). There is something beautiful and intimate about
this. If our kids object to our kissing in the kitchen, in the
den, or anywhere else their curious eyes catch us in the
act, we respond in harmony, "We're married." This teaches
them on a monthly basis that certain acts of physical affection are rightly reserved for husband and wife.

The Biggest Benefit of NFP in Marriage

Abstinence is often the biggest hurdle for couples to overcome in using NFP. NFP users may have about as much

sex each month as most other people, but they don't get to have it whenever they want it. Ironically, abstinence is actually the biggest benefit of NFP in marriage. Willing abstinence says to your spouse, "I love you more than I love sex." It says, "I will sacrifice my needs and wants for you and for the greater good of the family."

Deferring lovemaking to the infertile times requires self-control and chastity, and those are good things! St. Augustine described chastity as follows: "Be subject to God, and your flesh subject to you. What more fitting! What more fair! You are subject to the higher and the lower is subject to you. . . . If you do not obey the Lord, you shall be tormented by your servant."[10] No one wants to be tormented by out-of-control sexual desire.

Ideally, people develop habits of chastity and abstinence in their teenage and young adult years and remain chaste during the engagement period. In the real world, it doesn't always happen this way. But premarital abstinence and periodic abstinence within marriage share some bedrock similarities. Premarital abstinence sends the message that you're worth waiting for. Periodic abstinence in marriage sends the message that you're still worth waiting for. Or, as Manny reassures me, "You're my wife, not a provider of orgasms."

People who haven't practiced chastity in a long time or people suffering from porn addictions might find abstinence a more difficult habit to acquire. But as with all virtues, chastity improves with practice. Saying no to ourselves in one area might help us say no to ourselves in other areas. Habits of sexual self-control can therefore aid in defeating a porn addiction (although counseling and twelve-step programs are frequently also required). In short, rather than being a burden, the abstinence required by NFP can be a blessing.

NFP and Achieving Pregnancy

Another advantage to NFP is that it can be used to achieve pregnancy, not just avoid it. The Church recognizes that "couples who discover that they are sterile suffer greatly" (*CCC*, 2374). In vitro fertilization (IVF) is the most common means of assisted reproductive technology, but it is not the only available treatment for infertility.

The effectiveness of NFP in helping couples to achieve pregnancy is similar to success rates of IVF. In vitro fertilization has an approximately 30 percent success rate, meaning that out of all cycles of treatment only 30 percent result in live births.[11] A study of infertility patients using NFP to achieve pregnancy reported a comparable success rate of about 28 percent.[12]

Compared to the average cost of IVF, which exceeds $10,000, treating infertility with NFP is far less expensive and does not involve selective reduction, a process that deliberately destroys one or more children in the womb and "reduces human life to the level of simple 'biological material' to be freely disposed of" (*EV*, 14).

In Search of Everlasting Love

Is There a Link between In Vitro Fertilization and Abortion?

David and Doreen, both agnostic, married young and used contraception for many years so they could build their respective careers. In their midthirties, they began trying to conceive a child without success. They turned to IVF at a price tag of nearly $20,000, only some of which was covered by insurance. Eleven embryos were created.

The day that two chosen embryos were implanted in her body seemed completely surreal to Doreen. On her back in a vinyl medical chair, her feet up in stirrups, Doreen lay quietly while the doctor moved quickly through the short procedure, using an instrument that looked like a turkey baster. Doreen described the experience as strange, clinical, impersonal, and "anticlimactic—not the way I expected a child to be conceived." About nine months later, she gave birth to twins.

David and Doreen paid $1,000 per year to store the remaining embryos for future use. They decided to undergo another cycle of treatments five years later. The doctors unfroze three embryos, selected the best one, and discarded the other two. The implantation succeeded, but Doreen miscarried the baby. A few years later, David and Doreen began having marital problems and, in part to avoid the ongoing costs of storage, decided to donate the remaining six embryos to science.

Reflection Questions

1. What was Doreen's emotional response to in vitro fertilization?

2. What was David's role in the fertilization?

3. Was there a link between the couple's use of contraception, in vitro fertilization, and the eventual embryo destruction?

Manny's Diagnosis

Doreen was bothered by the impersonal experience of in vitro fertilization, even though she didn't have any religious objection to it. David's role in becoming a father was distant almost from the start. The couple's choice to delay having children and their subsequent infertility were emotionally difficult for both of them. Continuing medical expenses to store the frozen embryos and Doreen's inability to carry the later pregnancy to term put a further strain on the marriage. Because the procreative and unitive functions of sex were separated, the experience of bringing a child into the world became a kind of medical transaction for the couple, rather than an intimate gift of love. Conceived through science, the embryos were abandoned as biomedical waste rather than cherished as tiny human beings.

Although assisted reproductive technologies such as IVF seem to be at the service of life, they in fact open the door to new threats against life. This is one of the primary reasons the Church opposes techniques such as IVF, artificial insemination, pregnancies created through donated sperm or eggs, and surrogate motherhood (*CCC*, 2376–2377). The *Catechism* explains that in artificial reproductive techniques, "the act which brings the child into existence is no longer an act by which two persons give themselves to one another, but one that 'entrusts the life and identity of the embryo into the power of doctors and biologists and establishes the domination of technology over the origin and destiny of the human person'" (*CCC*, 2377).

Ultimately speaking, a child is a person to be welcomed into your family and your heart, not an object that can be purchased or demanded as a right. "A child is not something *owed* to one, but is a *gift*" (*CCC*, 2378).

Selecting the Right Method of NFP for You

Some couples choose not to use NFP at all. Friends of ours with four kids merrily announced, "Oh, we never planned anything!" Some couples don't struggle with their fertility. But many, many couples do. NFP can be a godsend for struggling couples, but as we said earlier, it really matters what method you select. Every method does not work equally well for every couple at every stage in their lives.

The different methods of NFP build on a basic knowledge of the female reproductive system to teach couples how to observe and chart the biomarkers that signal fertile and infertile times. NFP methods vary according to which biomarker they track most closely. Some methods track mainly basal body temperature and cervical mucus, some methods track cervical mucus only, and more recent methods use over-the-counter ovulation tests plus observations of cervical mucus. We've tried all these different types and will discuss them in the order that we used them.

Basal Body Temperature plus Cervical Mucus

This method is known as the sympto-thermal method and is taught by the Couple to Couple League (www .ccli.org). The two main biomarkers that are observed in this method are the woman's basal body temperature and her cervical mucus. Basal body temperature is taken and recorded at the beginning of the day, and the most fertile mucus characteristic is recorded at the end of the day. The basal body temperature reading is most accurate when it's taken after three to six hours of sleep and at the same time every day.

The sympto-thermal method was the first type of NFP we tried. It didn't work well for us because we started it

when our first baby was only a few months old and my
sleep patterns were inconsistent at best. (Incidentally, this
is one big reason that pre-Cana teachers advise learning
NFP *before* the wedding and definitely before you think
you need it.) Many breast-fed newborns need to be nursed
every two to four hours, making longer stretches of sleep
impossible. Plus, our baby Lelia struggled a lot learning
to breast-feed. When I wasn't nursing, I was pumping.
Sleep was a far-off and distant memory.

I tried to take my basal body temperature after my
longest period of sleep even if the clock read 2:00 a.m. one
day and 9:00 a.m. the next. Not surprisingly, the charts
never showed a consistent pattern. As the months went
by and my menstruation didn't return, we realized that
the constant breast-feeding was preventing ovulation.
My temperature didn't reveal a menstrual cycle because
there wasn't one.

Ecological Breast-Feeding

Constant breast-feeding is actually its own kind of NFP.
The basics are simple: nurse the baby on demand, day
or night, and ovulation will be suppressed. How long it
works depends on each woman's biology. Over time, we
discovered that if we followed the one guideline of feeding on demand, day or night, my menstruation stopped
for a year or more.

The method fit well with our lifestyle. As a stay-at-
home mom, I was always available to nurse. Nursing
the baby in bed at night, also called co-sleeping, meant
no-fuss nighttime feedings. The baby would latch on and
I would doze off. We sometimes put the baby in a bassi-
net or crib in our bedroom when we wanted the bed to
ourselves. We didn't mind taking the baby everywhere
with us, to church, the store, or even on dates. The method

was free and required no cycle tracking and no abstinence whatsoever.

We used ecological breast-feeding for about six years in order to space our children two years apart. Then, at age thirty-seven, when I thought surely my fertility was diminishing, I got pregnant on the first ovulation before my cycle even returned. When the doctor asked for the last date of menstruation, I had to write a date that was more than twenty-four months prior. It was as if I had the gestation period of an elephant. After that, we decided to get more serious about avoiding another pregnancy.

Cervical Mucus Only

We chose the Creighton Model Fertility Care System (www.creightonmodel.com), one of the two primary mucus-only methods of NFP (the other is the Billings Method). We began Creighton classes six months post-partum and quickly ran into difficulties. Although some women have almost no cervical mucus while breast-feeding, others produce it continuously. I fell into the continuous camp, which meant according to the Creighton Model I was constantly fertile and couldn't have relations. Although convinced that my ovulation was suppressed because of ecological breast-feeding, we refrained from having sex since we didn't want a repeat pregnancy on the first ovulation before regaining my cycle.

I even weaned the baby earlier than usual, hoping to decrease mucus production. Although the mucus didn't stop, it began to vacillate between what I called supermucus, which had fertility characteristics so off the chart that it seemed we could populate a small planet, and mucus whose fertility characteristics were somewhat more restrained. Figuring that I could get pregnant only during the times of supermucus, we of course wound up welcoming our sixth little bundle of joy approximately nine months later, just before my fortieth birthday.

We considered breast-feeding our newest daughter until kindergarten at least to take advantage of the ovulation-suppressing characteristics of ecological breast-feeding. Alas, my cycle returned before her second birthday. We decided to go high tech and give ovulation testing a try.

Ovulation Test plus Mucus

The main method for ovulation testing is called the Marquette Model, developed at Marquette University in Milwaukee, Wisconsin (http://nfp.marquette.edu). The Marquette Model can be used with a fertility monitor only, mucus observation only, or monitor plus mucus. The model uses the ClearBlue Easy Fertility Monitor, available in drugstores, to measure two hormones in the urine—estrogen and luteinizing hormone (LH).

We didn't actually spring for the pricey fertility monitor, especially since we would still have to purchase test sticks regularly. Instead, we used bargain-basement test strips from the local pharmacy. Together with a free cycle-tracking app that we downloaded for our smartphone, these ovulation tests plus cervical mucus observation have worked like a charm for us.

NFP resources have proliferated recently as more people are becoming aware of NFP's effectiveness for both achieving and avoiding pregnancy. In addition to in-person classes, many instructors are willing to teach long distance via phone, e-mail, or Skype. Some of the major methods offer home-study courses or video courses with individualized follow-up. Online charting is frequently available. Officially sanctioned smartphone apps have been released or are currently in development. Many fertility-tracking apps on the market also claim to be compatible with the major NFP methods. In short, it's easier than ever to learn an NFP method that fits with your lifestyle and is right for you.

Bonus Material

Conversation Starters

- Do you and your spouse agree on the morality of contraception? If you don't, how do you cope with this disagreement?
- What have you heard (good and bad) about NFP?
- Do you know anyone who uses NFP? Have you used NFP?
- Which NFP method do you think might work best for you and why?

Action Plan

Sit down and have a talk about different methods of family planning. If you're not already using NFP, you may wish to consider prayerfully whether you would like to switch to NFP for medical or moral reasons.

Catechism Corner

Methods of natural family planning "respect the bodies of the spouses, encourage tenderness between them, and favor the education of an authentic freedom" (*CCC*, 2370).

9.

Turning Challenges into Channels of Grace

BIG FAMILIES, SPECIAL-NEEDS KIDS, ADOPTING, FOSTERING, AND STEPPARENTING

> The family is a community which provides help,
> which celebrates life and is fruitful. . . . Our voices
> are many, and . . . each is unique.
>
> —Pope Francis, Message for the Forty-Ninth World
> Communications Day

Every path to parenthood is unique, and every couple faces its own challenges. New parents sometimes tell us, "I don't know how you can raise six kids. We only have one, and it's so difficult for us!" We usually respond, "One *is* difficult." The transformation from loving spouses into caring parents will entail both joy and sorrow. Just as joy is rooted in the Cross, fruitfulness often stems from self-sacrifice (see Jn 12:24). And yet we can attest to the fact that no matter what kind of hardship we've faced or sacrifice we've been asked to make, God's grace *has* been sufficient (see 2 Cor 12:9).

Manny and I feel blessed to be surrounded by every-day heroes who have shown astonishing strength of character as they've faced extraordinary parenting challenges. Whereas we have six kids, many of our friends have more—into the double digits. Several of our friends have children with a range of special needs, including autism, Down syndrome, and muscular dystrophy.

We have watched other friends struggle with the cross of infertility and then turn that cross into a blessing by adopting or fostering children in need (although becoming adoptive or foster parents does not automatically go hand in hand with infertility). Still other people we know have turned stepparenting into an act of selfless love. All these special family circumstances can open the door to a flood of graces from heaven to sustain parents in their holy and often incredibly arduous work.

Big, Beautiful Catholic Families

Large families are "a sign of God's blessing and the parents' generosity," applauds the *Catechism* (*CCC*, 2373). Many canonized saints have come from large families. The life of St. Frances Xavier Cabrini, the last of thirteen children, is a terrific argument in favor of having a large family. Mother Cabrini came to the United States in 1889 to aid the Italian immigrant community and founded numerous schools, hospitals, and orphanages (*LS*, 471–72). She was the first American citizen ever to become a canonized saint.

St. Catherine of Siena, too, came from a large family—she was the twenty-third child (out of twenty-four)! St. Catherine was instrumental in convincing Pope Gregory XI to remove the papal see from Avignon, France, and return it to Rome (*LS*, 171). She is one of thirty-three

Doctors of the Church, meaning the Church has proclaimed her to have both eminent learning and a high
degree of sanctity.

Large families aren't very common today, so they
frequently attract a lot of comments. Our family is fortu-
nate to live in a heavily Catholic area of Long Island, New
York, so many of the comments we receive are positive.
After seeing us with six little kids in tow, some people
tell us "God bless you!" or "You're so lucky!" Our friend
Phyllis greets us with a cry of "Look at that big, beautiful
Catholic family!"

But other folks seem downright shocked. Again and
again, we hear, "Are you done?" in a tone of incredulity.
This strikes me as particularly hilarious, since my grandmother always hated to be asked at the end of a meal if
she was done. "Am I a turkey?" she would retort in her
elegant Virginia accent. "A lady is never *done*. She has
had a sufficiency." So when someone asks if we're done
having children, I always have to bite my tongue to keep
from saying, "Am I a turkey?" Manny will joke that we're
trying to reestablish the Spanish Empire or at least grow
our own sports team.

It can be irritating to field the constant and often
intrusive personal questions. But behind people's curi-
osity, however poorly expressed, is often admiration and
a deep desire to understand the increasingly rare phe-
nomenon of a big family.

Sometimes, other people's attitudes about large
families aren't the only hurdles to overcome, and they
may not even be the largest hurdles. Internal doubts can
also plague parents striving to be open to having large
families. In a heart-to-heart talk with our friend Kristin, I admitted to her that I didn't feel cut out to raise a
large family. She looked me straight in the eye and said,
"Nobody does." She said that when you feel God has

called you to do something, you just have to do your best
and let God do the rest.

The most convincing proof of the value of large
families comes from parents whose many children have
already grown up. Our friend Connie, who has ten children, is thrilled whenever our son gives her a hug because
her sons have gotten older and she doesn't get "little
boy hugs" anymore. And she got especially teary at her
youngest child's First Communion because it was the last
one. Her nostalgia for things she won't experience again
with her own children helps us to appreciate our children
as they are now.

Special-Needs Children

Like raising a large family, raising special-needs children
requires "very special courage," recognized John Paul II
(*LF*, 16). "The Church is close to those married couples
who, with great anguish and suffering, willingly accept
gravely handicapped children," he wrote (*EV*, 63). "But
the Church firmly believes that human life, even if weak
and suffering, is always a splendid gift of God's goodness" (*FC*, 48).

God creates each child, including those born with
sickness or disabilities, "*to express fully his humanity*" and
to discover who he or she is as a person (*LF*, 9). Such a
discovery can be amazing, as Elizabeth Matthews found
from her autistic son, Patrick, the third of her ten children. Elizabeth wrote many letters to Patrick while he
was away at a school for special-needs children—letters
he may never be able to read. In one of them she said,
"The months go by, and it hasn't gotten any easier. It does
not take much to start tears flowing from the eyes of your
daddy or me. It seems so wrong to have you so far away
from home, and yet we trust that God will use all this
suffering for His honor and glory."[1]

Special-needs children can give their parents a beautiful opportunity for sacrifice, an opportunity to do good. Why God allows sickness and disability has always been a mystery, but the Bible gives us some answers. When Jesus saw a man blind from birth, his disciples asked him why the man was born blind. Jesus responded, "So that God's works might be revealed in him." Then Jesus restored the man's sight (see Jn 9:1–3, 6–7). We cannot heal the sick as Jesus did, but when we care for them, we reveal God's love to the world.

The *Catechism* states, "The family should live in such a way that its members learn to care and take responsibility for the young, the old, the sick, the handicapped, and the poor" (*CCC*, 2208). Having a special-needs child presents the opportunity to provide loving service for the sick within our own families. Our friends Liz and Kent Gilges lived a life of service to their eldest daughter, Elie, for ten years until Elie's death in 2004. The first child of six, Elie was diagnosed with a brain tumor when she was one year old; she was soon bedridden and uncommunicative.

Before Elie was born, Liz promised God on numerous occasions that she would make any sacrifice for the sake of her husband's soul, since he was agnostic. God clearly accepted Liz's sacrifice. Large numbers of people came to Elie's funeral, inspiring her father, Kent, not only to write a book about the deep value of Elie's life but also ultimately to enter the Catholic Church. The family next door saw the Gilgeses go to Mass every Sunday with Elie in a large wheelchair. Two years later the neighbors, who had never gone to any church, decided to convert to Catholicism. One friend of the Gilges family even became pregnant soon after praying for Elie's intercession to cure her infertility. Elie's life was, and continues to be, a blessing not only for her parents but for others as well.[2]

Sadly, parents who receive a prenatal diagnosis of disability often choose to abort their disabled child out of fear, rejecting the gift of his or her birth. But prenatal tests or screens aren't always accurate. Our friend Roberta took a routine AFP (alpha-fetoprotein) test while she was pregnant, and the test came back positive, indicating that the baby might have spina bifida. She and her husband worried a great deal before the baby was born and then discovered the test had been a false positive.

When the obstetrician asked if we wanted the same test when I was pregnant, we said no, afraid of experiencing something similar to what our friend had gone through. The obstetrician argued with our decision, but we asked him, "What would you do if the test turned out positive? Could you help the baby?" He said no, he would not be able to help the baby; he would simply inform us of the option to terminate pregnancy. Since abortion was not an option for us, we refused the test.

It takes courage and self-giving love for parents to receive an ill or handicapped child from the hand of God with faith and trust, refusing to turn a prenatal diagnosis into an opportunity for a "eugenic abortion" or a "death sentence" (*EV*, 14; *CCC*, 2274). Some statistics suggest that as many as 90 percent of children diagnosed with Down syndrome are aborted. Even though children with Down syndrome do tend to have greater needs and increased medical risks, these children can also bring great joy to their families. Listen to what our friends say about their daughter Margaret Rose:

> Margaret Rose, the youngest of our four children, has Down syndrome. We love her beyond description and feel blessed to have her in our lives. Her two sisters and brother argue over who gets to hug her first, hold her the longest, and play with her the most. . . . Maggie, who will be two next month,

is sweet, playful and affectionate. She possesses a
strong, almost stubborn will and has an abundance
of energy. . . . Her happiness is downright conta-
gious. . . . With love, life's problems don't detract
from happiness; they become an avenue through
which love finds expression, and it is in the act of
love that Maggie, like all of us, proves her worth.[3]

Parenting the Children of Your Heart

Every family images the Trinity, especially in its fruitfulness (*CCC*, 2205). In the Trinity, the love between the
Father and the Son is so powerful that it *is* another person—the Holy Spirit.[4] Analogously, in a family, the love
between a man and a woman is so powerful that it can
generate another person—a child. But as we said earlier
in the book, fertility is not only physical. Sometimes the
offspring of married love are not our biological sons and
daughters but are children of our hearts.

As Christians, we can extend our love beyond the
bonds of flesh and blood by recognizing that all human
beings are children of the same heavenly Father (*FC*, 41).
God calls some of us to welcome children into our families through adopting, fostering, or stepparenting.

Although the loss of the bond between the child and
his or her birth parents is real and may require special
help to process (particularly in older children), adoption
can also be a great blessing for all concerned. For the
adoptive parents, adoption can provide a joyous alternative for infertility treatments, such as in vitro fertilization,
which are discouraged by the Church (*CCC*, 2376–2377,
2379). By some reports, one in five couples in the United
States experiences at least temporary infertility. Almost
half of the couples we taught in our first pre-Cana class
unsuccessfully tried to conceive children in the first year

of their marriage. Some of them eventually turned to adoption to bring a child into their family.

Adopted children, in turn, receive the blessing of a loving family willing to serve them in the way that Jesus taught in the gospels: "For I was hungry and you gave me food, I was thirsty and you gave me something to drink, I was a stranger and you welcomed me" (Mt 25:35; *LF*, 22). Fostering or adopting an older child, or a child with physical or emotional challenges, fulfills this call in a unique way.

Birth parents should also be recognized for their courageous and sacrificial choices, for putting their child's needs ahead of their own. As Timothy O'Malley pointed out in his article in *America* magazine, "The process of adopting is an act of human love, of self-gift, between strangers who are bonded together in the mystery of divine love for the very same child. And in this mutual self-gift, a child does not simply come into physical existence, but instead dwells in a family of love that stretches biological bounds."[5]

Like most worthy deeds, adoption can be challenging. This holds particularly true when adopting older children or children who have experienced trauma, or when trying to blend adopted children and biological children into one family. One Long Island couple with six biological children went on to adopt four special-needs children: a four-year-old with tiptoe syndrome, a two-year-old with cerebral palsy, a child less than a year old with herpes and syphilis, and a newborn with a heart murmur, one working kidney, and other developmental defects. The father said, "This is what we were placed on this world to do, raise a large family, including these children with special needs. We stand proud. This is our vocation; it's not for everyone but it is for us."

In Search of Everlasting Love

What Fulfillment Can Couples Find through Becoming Adoptive Parents?

Rick and Jeanine were married for eight years and were unable to conceive children, so they decided to adopt a baby girl from China. After they began the adoption process, Jeanine became pregnant and gave birth to a daughter about the same age as their adopted daughter. Two years later, Jeanine and Rick had another child, this time a baby boy.

Their adopted daughter, Siu-lin, suffered from reactive attachment disorder from the neglect she suffered in China. Siu-lin only rarely showed affection. Nothing soothed her frequent temper tantrums. Staying calm and continuing to show steady love and affection to Siu-lin took a heavy emotional toll on Rick and especially Jeanine, who felt incapable of parenting Siu-lin successfully. In therapy, Jeanine received constant encouragement and praise, in addition to medication for her depression. By age eleven, Siu-lin developed into a respectful and loving girl who achieved good grades in school and related well to her parents and her peers.

Reflection Questions

1. How did Rick and Jeanine make a difference in Siu-lin's life?

2. How did Jeanine benefit from parenting Siu-lin?

3. What if Siu-lin's attachment disorder had not been resolved?

Manny's Diagnosis

Rick and Jeanine were able to give Siu-lin the care and affection that she had not received while in the orphanage in China. Through her perseverance in caring for Siu-lin, Jeanine was able to find reservoirs of inner strength that she did not realize she had. This perseverance, combined with the grace of God, led to Siu-lin's successful adjustment.

Rick and Jeanine were so grateful to see the difference their efforts had made. Sadly, many children do not recover from neglect in infancy. Attachment problems can become a lifelong cross. But God's grace gives us the strength to bear the crosses we've been given.

Adopting a child in need does not always mean taking the child into your home. The Church encourages "adoption at a distance" when the only reason for adoption is the extreme poverty of the child's parents (*EV*, 93). Our friends Jennifer and Phil regularly send money for the care of a boy named Asadd, whom they met while Phil was studying medicine in Grenada, West Indies. When they first met Asadd, his mother was young, single, impoverished, and in need of help, so Jennifer and Phil considered legally adopting Asadd. The boy's birth father fought the adoption, however, and then Jennifer and Phil had to move back to the United States. Jennifer and Phil stayed in contact with Asadd, sending him money and supplies when he needed it and always keeping him in their prayers.

Foster care is another way for married couples to serve life (see *FC*, 41). Tammy and Richard became interested in foster parenting when they heard a talk at

Mass promoting it. At the time, their ninth child had just turned three years old. After fostering two infants for brief periods of time, they took in two sisters under the age of two, whom they were eventually able to adopt when their mother's rights were terminated due to an ongoing drug addiction. Next they fostered a little boy, T, who came into their home when he was one day old because his mother was incarcerated. Although he has auditory processing problems, learning disabilities, and severe obsessive-compulsive disorder, Tammy and Richard eventually adopted T as well, since theirs was the only home he had ever known. Why did these parents, who already had nine biological children, decide to foster and then adopt three more children? "We felt we had more to give," said Tammy.

Stepparenting, too, involves opening your heart generously—in this case, to the children your spouse had with another person. And whereas nature gives us nine or so months to get used to the idea of becoming a parent, stepparenting is instantaneous. You are a parent the moment you leave the altar.

Our friend Wilfrid tells a truly inspiring story about his stepmother—his "second mother." Wilfrid was one of eight children under eleven years of age when they lost their mother. Well-meaning friends and neighbors encouraged Wilfrid's father to foster the children with several different families in the parish. Wilfrid's father refused and kept the family together for two years, with the help of an aunt, until he found Wilfrid's stepmother, Leontine. Leontine was eager to step in and raise the eight children as her own.

My sister-in-law Becky likewise opened her arms and her heart to Andi, my brother's daughter from his first marriage. Even while Becky was dating my brother, she would help bathe my niece and put her to bed. Becky's parents accepted the little girl as their first granddaughter without blinking an eye. Sitting around the family table one year for Andi's birthday celebration, we all watched Andi burst into tears because Becky had bought her the absolutely perfect birthday gift, paying for rush shipping to make sure Andi got it in time for her party. In that moment (and many others), Becky exemplified true motherly love.

No matter what form our families take, they are an expression of God's love and fruitfulness. They are at the service of human life, which is "always a splendid gift of God's goodness" (*FC*, 48).

Bonus Material

Conversation Starters

- What particular challenges do you think large families or blended families face? What families do you know who have managed such challenges successfully?
- Do you have friends whose children have special needs? What strikes you about the role the child plays in the family?
- Do you have friends who have chosen to adopt or foster a child? What have you learned from them about what it means to be a family?
- Have you considered adopting or fostering children? What about special-needs children? Do you feel called to have a large family, or a larger one than you have now?

Action Plan

Say a prayer for families in special circumstances. If your family members or friends are facing these circumstances, call them and tell them how much you admire them. Offer to take care of the children for an evening to give the parents some well-deserved time alone together. And consider whether God is calling you to expand your family by adoption, fostering, or having another child.

Catechism Corner

"The family should live in such a way that its members learn to care and take responsibility for the young, the old, the sick, the handicapped, and the poor" (*CCC*, 2208).

PART IV

CALLED TO LOVE
TOTALLY AND FOREVER

Nurturing Faith from
Generation to Generation

The final key to everlasting love is a willingness to give every part of yourself (totally) for the rest of your life (forever). Just as God wants to shower us with every good thing, we are called to spend our earthly lives sharing all we have and all we are with our spouse, our family, and our God. We are called to a total, radical gift of self.

As a reminder of this call to self-surrender, our relatives Fran and Nancy inscribed the Latin words *Totus Tuus* ("all yours") on the inside of their wedding bands. This motto of John Paul II's pontificate expressed his desire to dedicate himself totally to Christ through the Virgin Mary. What a beautiful way for a married couple to show their ardent desire to dedicate themselves totally to Christ through each other, to say, "Here I am, and I am all yours!"

Even the best marriage will last only a lifetime. But through our children, our love can extend generation upon generation. We pass on our values, ethics, and faith to the children we raise. They, in turn, are witnesses to the broader world. In our mission as parents and spouses, we can look to the Holy Family to show us the way. Joseph and Mary had a true marriage with all the characteristics of everlasting love. They freely consented to God's plan, they were faithful to each other, their marriage bore immense spiritual fruit through their son, Jesus, and they never abandoned one another by divorce (*Redemptoris Custos* [*RC*], 7). They surrendered themselves totally to each other and to the amazing power of God.

When you give your all to God, he alone can give you everything in return: all patience, kindness, gentleness, and vitality. He alone can fill you with a divine spousal love so you can love one another the way that he has loved you. When you give yourself totally to your spouse in your joy and in your sorrow, and when you accept your spouse totally with his or her strengths and flaws, then you have learned the final key to everlasting love.

10.

Turning Children into Adults

FORMING YOUR CHILDREN'S BODIES, MINDS, AND SOULS IN CHRIST

Education consists essentially in preparing man for what he must be and for what he must do here below, in order to attain the sublime end for which he was created.

—Pope Pius XI, *Divini Illius Magistri*, 7

When I became pregnant with our first child, we had very few friends with children and almost no idea what to expect. Oma and Opa told us, "It will be really hard—the hardest thing you've ever done." We would smile dreamily in reply. "Oh, we know."

In reality, we were completely clueless.

Babies are soft, warm, and sweet. They are also incredibly helpless, furiously loud, constantly hungry, and occasionally smelly. And that's just the first few months. Babies are Responsibility with a capital *R*. Our children's bodies can last one hundred years or more. Their minds influence not only their own futures but those of countless generations to follow. And their souls last forever.

If we are like pencils in the hands of God, as Mother Teresa said, then each of our children is a sketch destined to become a masterpiece. Our job as parents is to help our children achieve their God-given potential. "Parents have the most grave duty and primary right to take care as best they can for the physical, social, cultural, moral, and religious education of their offspring."[1] (And you probably thought your day job was hard.)

Being a good parent requires total commitment. But don't be afraid—with the gift of each child, God grants to those who ask for it the strength to do what needs to be done. (Plus, after you have your third or fourth child, you get a lot more relaxed about the whole thing.)

Unity is as crucial in parenting as it is in marriage. There are a thousand different ways to parent a child well, but the two of you need to agree on the way that works best for you. You can choose breast-feeding or bottle-feeding, spanking or time-outs, attachment parenting or live-in nannies or day care, and homeschooling or Catholic schooling or public schooling. But you need to make the choices together.

Although it can be helpful to seek insight from other parents who have been there, ultimately it doesn't matter what every other parent at the playground picks. There will never be one parenting style that is objectively correct and applies to everyone. Because every mother, father, child, and family is unique, no family functions exactly the same. There is no reason it should. As long as, before God, you and your husband are doing your best to meet the physical, emotional, and spiritual needs of the children he has entrusted to you, be at peace.

Developing a parenting style that works for your family may be difficult at first. Some of the issues that create the greatest conflict between spouses arise only after they have been married five or ten years, when they are focused on child rearing. Parenting styles and differences in religious practice are high on the list. If you have unresolved issues about how you were raised, you may find them resurfacing as your children go through similar stages. You may find yourself wanting to copy what your parents did or wanting to do the opposite. Your spouse will probably be going through the same thought process. Non-Catholic spouses may want to pass their religious traditions down to their children, even though the Catholic spouses promised to raise their children Catholic.

As children grow older, they'll notice and exploit any differences in opinion. If Mom says no, they'll ask Dad, and vice versa. Get used to saying things like, "Did you already ask your mother?" or, "Mom and Dad will have to talk it over first, and when we've made our decision, we'll let you know." Communication and bonding will be essential as never before.

Caring for Your Children's Bodies

A baby's complete physical dependence can turn new parents' worlds upside down, particularly if they are unprepared for it. But when we take care of our children's physical needs, we are showing them the depth of our love (*CCC*, 2228).

Back in 1929, Pope Pius XI lamented that while people devoted many hours to career training and professional development, "for the fundamental duty and obligation of educating their children, many parents have little or no preparation" (*Divini Illius Magistri* [*DIM*], 73–74). I was guilty as charged. Before our first child, Lelia, was born, my life revolved around my work as a litigator in a law firm housed in a towering black skyscraper in Midtown Manhattan. Breakfast was a bagel from the cart on the corner, lunch was from the deli down the block, and dinner was Chinese takeout or part of a night out on the town. There were no dishes to wash and no groceries to buy; a maid did the laundry and cleaned the apartment, where I spent very little time.

My lack of preparation hit like a ton of bricks on my first day of maternity leave. In one fell swoop, I went from barely lifting a finger to take care of myself to tending to *three* people (our infant daughter, my husband, and me) in an apartment with four walls I scarcely recognized. Breast-feeding turned out to be a terrible and complicated ordeal, and we forked over hundreds of dollars to lactation consultants. For the first six weeks the pattern continued, all day and all night: it would take thirty minutes to feed Lelia; then an hour later she would wake, screaming with hunger again.

In the midst of my exhausted haze, the words of the sacrifice of the Mass began to take on an intimate connection to my daily life. "This is my body which is given up for you." I was giving my body to God by embracing motherhood regardless of the cost to my career or other personal ambitions. "Take this and eat it. This is my body." I was also offering my body to my baby daughter, asking her to take and eat, giving to her body nourishment and life. This was the great and splendid parenting ministry that St. Thomas Aquinas had compared to the ministry of priests (*FC*, 38). If it had not come with so much struggle and sacrifice, I might have missed its significance entirely.

Unconsciously, I had expected my child to cooperate with my routine, as if she were a machine. The unrelenting demand of Lelia's physical needs rescued me from my mistaken worldviews and contributed to my own growth in holiness (see *CCC*, 2227). As we raise our children, God the Father raises us up, too.

Caring for Your Children's Minds

Parents of young children often imagine that because the children can feed, bathe, read to, and clothe themselves, the children's school years will be a relative oasis of rest. And yet, this is rarely the case. As Oma's mother, a mom of five, mused, "It's not easier. Just . . . different." As children grow, their needs for mental, social, and spiritual stimulation increase, requiring far more than simply correcting the occasional error in homework and driving them to extracurricular activities.

The parents' role in their children's education is indispensable (*CCC*, 2221; *DIM*, 71). John Paul II declared, *"Parents are the first and most important educators* of their own children. . . . All other participants in the process of education are only able to carry out their responsibilities *in the name of the parents"* (*LF*, 16).

We found out early on that if our children were not first exposed to knowledge at home, they could not learn well at school. We had to teach them *how* to study and budget their time to complete long-term projects. Even in the early years of education, learning how to read requires a lot of one-on-one attention that schools cannot always provide. Seeing the major national monuments in the pages of a book is no substitute for visiting them in person during a family outing or vacation. What kids learn at home is reinforced by what they learn at school, not necessarily the other way around.

Teachers are experts in education, but you are an expert in your own children. You know better than anyone what they need and what they are capable of accomplishing. Your children have each been given their own unique talents. It's up to you to discover those talents and make them grow.

Parents are like the stewards in Jesus' parable of the talents. In this well-known parable, the property owner entrusted different numbers of talents, coins worth more than fifteen years of a laborer's wages, to his stewards. "To one he gave five talents, to another two, to another one, to each according to his ability" (Mt 25:15). The steward with five talents invested his money wisely and increased his five talents to ten. The steward with two talents also doubled his money from two talents to four. But the steward with one talent buried it in the ground in fear. When the owner returned, he was pleased with the stewards who had doubled what they had been given but displeased with the one who had left his talent unused (see Mt 25:14–30).

Parents are stewards of their children's talents when the children are young and in the parents' care. It's important to face the reality that not all children have equal talents. We cannot expect more intellectual accomplishments from our children than they can realistically achieve. But we must also not leave our children's talents buried where they cannot be dug up without our help. Look beyond aptitudes for reading and math and discover whether your child has a talent for art, nature, music, or sports. Extracurricular activities, books, magazines, and even entire television channels exist to help nurture diverse talents.

To develop Lelia's artistic talents, we enrolled her in professional art classes, purchased art textbooks to expose her to the rich tradition of religious art, and supplied her with scraps of cloth and trim. To encourage Miguel's interest in nature, we checked out nonfiction books and nature documentaries from the library and amassed a fantastic collection of fish, frogs, toads, turtles, and lizards.

We allowed Maria, who gets straight As without breaking a sweat, to set up a school for her younger siblings in the basement. And we ferry Marguerite and Cecilia back and forth to competitive gymnastics meets where they regularly earn medals. Emma will have her turn soon.

In addition to spotting and encouraging your children's natural talents, it's also important to recognize when they struggle more than they ought. There are 2.4 million American public school students identified as having one or more learning disabilities, with many more remaining undiagnosed. Autistic spectrum disorders and attention deficit disorder are both on the rise.[2] Although educational support services exist, it can be a titanic struggle to receive them from overburdened school districts concerned about budgets.

We experienced this with our daughter Lelia, who struggled mightily with reading in kindergarten. Homework inexplicably took her twice as long as the recommended time, a problem that continued through first and second grade. As her workload increased, so did our frustration.

Over time it became clear that Lelia's struggle did not stem primarily from lack of interest or lack of motivation. Her brain just worked differently. After we explained concepts to her sometimes in three or four different ways, especially if we used diagrams or pictures, it would suddenly click. Two years of educational testing finally resulted in a diagnosis of attention deficit hyperactivity disorder (ADHD). Finally, with a diagnosis in our pocket, the school became willing to offer us accommodations such as additional help with test taking and a reduced homework load.

Deciding how and where to school a struggling child is simply one more prudential decision all parents must make—there really are no right or wrong answers across the board. Depending on the resources available in your local school district, you may decide on public or charter schools, private or Catholic schools, or some form of homeschooling. There is no need to lock all your children into one approach or one school system. Some parents switch their kids from private or public schooling to homeschooling and then back again. The one thing that parents ought not to do is let the importance of intellectual education overshadow moral education.

In Search of Everlasting Love

Can Parents Overemphasize Intellectual Development at the Expense of Moral Development?

Tim and Susan lived on Manhattan's Lower East Side. Susan worked as a secretary, and Tim worked as a paralegal. They both felt underemployed and wanted their only son, Henry, to have opportunities that were unavailable to them. Though it was a struggle to pay the tuition, they decided to enroll Henry in an intellectually rigorous and very expensive private high school.

The other children at the high school came from wealthy families. As the school year ended, Henry asked to attend an exclusive summer camp with his friends and became bitter and angry when his parents refused. He did not know that his parents couldn't afford the summer camp and that the school itself was straining their resources. They felt guilty for having to tell him no. Sinking under the weight of their financial troubles, Susan became depressed.

Reflection Questions

1. How did Tim and Susan's feelings of professional inadequacy affect the choice of schooling for their son?

2. Why didn't they want to admit their financial situation to their son?

3. Was the financial sacrifice made by Tim and Susan to send their son to such an expensive school helping or hindering Henry's moral development?

Manny's Diagnosis

Many parents want their children to have a better life than they had. But sometimes parents have a narcissistic desire to make their children's success a substitute for their own. Tim and Susan were trying to succeed through their son in areas in which they felt like failures. Their sense of self-worth was unhealthily dependent on what their son thought of them, which is why they didn't want to admit their real financial situation to him.

Tim and Susan were advised not to hide the financial sacrifices they were making to pay for Henry's private school tuition. Henry needed to recognize and value the opportunities they were providing for him. Tim and Susan were also encouraged not to feel obligated to give their son the same things that his friends had and to consider other education options if he continued to be bitter, angry, and unappreciative for the well-being of the whole family.

The Church has always supported a high degree of intellectual learning, as evidenced by the large networks of Catholic schools and universities throughout the country.

But a truly Christian education "takes in the whole aggregate of human life, physical and spiritual, intellectual and moral . . . in order to elevate, regulate and perfect it, in accordance with the example and teaching of Christ" (*DIM*, 47, 95).

Intellectual development should not be emphasized above all else. The canonized saints of the Church include the not so smart as well as the phenomenally brilliant. St. Peter will not require us to show a school report card with straight As in order to pass through the gates of heaven.

St. Bernadette is a fabulous example of a saint who wasn't particularly gifted intellectually. She was ridiculed by both her teachers and fellow schoolchildren for her poor memory. And yet our Blessed Mother chose to appear to St. Bernadette at what became the world-famous healing shrine in Lourdes, France, and St. Bernadette turned out to be one of the Church's most widely known and beloved saints. When we become overly concerned about our children's academic performance, St. Bernadette's example helps us to remember that God will work his purpose out in our children regardless of whether the world sees them as superstars or not.

Caring for Your Children's Souls

The work of parents is not only to turn their children into adults but also to turn them into saints. Parental responsibility "cannot be reduced solely to the procreation of children," states the *Catechism*, "but must extend to their moral education and their spiritual formation" (*CCC*, 2221). Care of your children's souls has such fundamental importance that the priest asks during the Rite of Marriage, "Will you accept children lovingly from God, and bring them up according to the law of Christ and his Church?"

No religion teacher or catechist can weave the teachings of the Bible into the fabric of your children's lives as you can (*CCC*, 2226; *LF*, 16). By teaching kids to pray and bringing them to the sacraments, parents can infuse children "from their tenderest years with the life of the Church" (*CCC*, 2225). Almost every question that your children ask about friendship, sharing, or any type of human relationship can be answered by a quote or story from the Bible.

But because grace builds on nature, you also bring your children closer to God when you encourage them to develop their naturally good tendencies. For example, most children want to please their parents and make them happy. Obedience flows naturally from a desire to please. Obedience has gotten a bad rap these days, as if parents have no right to insist upon it. But it's included in the Ten Commandments. For children, *honoring* their father and mother according to the fourth commandment means *obeying* their father and mother (*CCC*, 2214). One of the best things you can do to raise your children well is to teach them what is right and then ensure that they do it.

Obedience flourishes where there is consistent discipline. As the child matures, the flower of obedience bears the fruit of self-discipline if parents take time to explain the reasons behind the rules. Without an explanation, kids often misunderstand the motivation for a particular action, complaining that "Daddy is mean" or "Mommy just likes to punish me." While transmitting our values, we need to take time to explain them. Kids may not immediately and fully grasp what we are saying at first, but with each explanation they come to trust that we have important reasons for acting as we do.

Children respond best to discipline when they know they are encouraged and loved, and they resist it when a parent is constantly harsh and critical. So it's important to catch your child being good. For example, if you criticize your children for selfish behavior, make an extra effort to praise them when you see them sharing generously without complaint. This strengthens your relationship and your parental authority. This is especially important as children get older—when teens obey not because you are bigger and smarter than they are but because they know you want what is best for them.

When Jesus became a tween, he proved his independence by remaining in the temple in Jerusalem by himself for three days. Afterward he returned to live in Nazareth and remained "obedient" to Joseph and Mary (see Lk 2:51). Jesus did not obey his parents because they had greater resources or superior strength. He obeyed them out of honor and love.

Especially as children get older and more self-sufficient, parents need to merit the obedience of their children, explained John Paul II (*LF*, 15). St. Thérèse of Lisieux said that her parents' loving tenderness made her want to respond cheerfully and obediently so she could show them how much she loved them in return, according to her autobiography, *The Story of a Soul*. Within a loving family, parents and children serve one another in a constant give and take. The goal of a family is not parents giving all and children taking all, nor is it children giving all and parents taking all. The goal is *mutual service* (*FC*, 21).

Two Virtues for Living

In addition to teaching children the value of obedience and mutual service, parents are called to give children an *"education in the virtues"* (*CCC*, 2223). There are so many virtues that it's impossible to list them, but two particular virtues that John Paul II thought parents should teach their children are antimaterialism and chastity, or modesty (*FC*, 37).

Materialism means treating things as more important than people. Antimaterialism means realizing that "man is more precious for what he is than for what he has" (*FC,* 37). Unfortunately, particularly around birthdays and holidays, parents frequently overemphasize the importance of things such as toys. In our years as young parents, we were no exception.

When Lelia was two years old, we planned a humdinger of a Christmas (having nothing to do with the religious meaning of the holiday at all). We bought her lots and lots of gifts, and so did her grandparents and aunts and uncles. The pièce de résistance was a battery-operated Dora the Explorer dollhouse in brightly colored plastic with more than thirty-five pieces and costing more than $100. We carefully orchestrated the Christmas gift opening to lead up to this final giant gift. However, Lelia became so worn out opening all the other presents that she barely glanced at the magnificent dollhouse.

We vowed never to indulge in such excessive gift giving again. But we still hadn't completely learned our lesson. For Lelia's third birthday, we planned to take her to Manhattan for a Broadway-style show for kids at Radio City Music Hall, in addition to having a several-hours-long family party at our house the day before. Regrettably, halfway through the Radio City show, Lelia got so overexcited that she vomited all over the heads of the people sitting in front of us. Embarrassed beyond words, we ran out of the theater as fast as possible without a word of apology to our unfortunate fellow theatergoers. The moral of this story is that excessive materialism (and the overstimulation that often results) makes kids nauseated, not happy!

Materialism is a little like immodesty. Materialism overvalues things and undervalues people. Immodesty overvalues physical attractiveness and undervalues inner worth. When we teach children to value their relationships with people—"body, emotions and soul" (*FC*, 37)—and put a higher value on time spent with them than the things they receive, children will discover that their own value is based not on what they produce but on who they are. The virtue of modesty helps children to see the true beauty of the human person—a beauty that is based not on a physical ideal but on a right ordering of the body, soul, and spirit.

As St. Thomas More wrote to his daughters' tutor, "Warn my children . . . to walk in the pleasant meadows of modesty; . . . not to think more of themselves for gaudy trappings, nor less for the want of them; neither to deform the beauty that nature has given them by neglect, nor to try to heighten it by artifice."[3] Children need examples of real beauty in their lives. If the only icon of beauty that children ever see is the latest pop star, they will never learn to imitate or to seek out tasteful elegance. Opa's mother always dressed beautifully and modestly. At her eightieth birthday party, she wore a dramatic red and black velvet cocktail dress. With her pearl necklace and cloud of white hair, she was the best-looking woman there.

Opa's mother taught me that flashiness is not ultimately what a man looks for in a woman. She also taught my brother that dressing and acting as a gentleman shows proper respect toward a lady; in fact, she insisted that he never visit her without wearing a jacket and tie, and he complied with her request.

The way we dress communicates an essential message to the people around us. It communicates how we feel about ourselves, how we feel about others, and what kind of relationships we're open to. "Slovenly dress" shows disrespect to the people around us, wrote St. Francis de Sales. "I should like my devout man or woman to be the best-dressed person" in the room, without being gaudy or ostentatious, he added.[4] An appreciation for beauty and a care for the details of our appearance can demonstrate an appreciation for ourselves, the people around us, and God as the author of human beauty.

Respect for human beauty leads girls to respect themselves and leads boys to respect girls. This attitude can radically influence the choices that boys and girls make in their lives, in whom they choose as their friends, as their boyfriends and girlfriends, and ultimately as their spouses.

Caring for the Children of God

Your children are not just your children. They are also the sons and the daughters of God (*CCC*, 2222). They are vulnerable and, as some of the least among us, deserve special care and protection from those who might harm them.

Rather horrifically, child protective services agencies received 3.4 million reports of child abuse or neglect involving 6.3 million children in 2012 alone. Out of 678,810 verified victims, more than 15 percent suffered from physical abuse and slightly fewer than 10 percent suffered from sexual abuse, with the rest being victims of neglect. Second only to parents, male relatives were the largest category of perpetrators.[5]

Sexual abuse is a particularly terrible type of abuse that endangers children's bodies, minds, and souls. "Sexual abuse occurs in all racial and cultural groups; in rural, suburban, and urban areas; and at all socioeconomic and educational levels. Authorities believe that many cases go unreported because they involve family or friends."[6]

Parents never want to hear that their child has been sexually abused, but many parents do confront this issue and it's important to know how to respond. First, the child should never be blamed or considered responsible for the abuse. Second, the abuser should be confronted and held accountable, even when the abuser is a fellow family member or trusted authority figure.[7] Immediate and intensive intervention through therapy is imperative for both victim and offender—particularly when the perpetrator is a child, as he or she may have been victimized as well. A qualified therapist can help the family decide the best way to protect all the children in the home—which in addition to intensive counseling may also include in-home safety plans, residential counseling, and alerting the proper authorities.

In Search of Everlasting Love

How Can Families Deal with Situations of Sexual Abuse?

Sam and Caroline had one daughter named Alexandra. Caroline's younger brother Philip was close to the family and spent a lot of time in the house. When Alexandra was fourteen years old, she complained to her mother that Uncle Philip had touched her inappropriately and tried to do more.

Caroline minimized the incident, not wanting to believe her brother was capable of such a thing. She blamed Alexandra for dressing provocatively in skimpy outfits and bikini bathing suits and reminded her of her tendency to exaggerate to stir up drama. Caroline did not confront Philip or bar his access from the house or even prevent Alexandra from being left alone with him—something she later deeply regretted.

When Alexandra was left alone in the house with her Uncle Philip, he would knock on her door and she would refuse to let him in. Sometimes, she hid in the basement. She began having thoughts of suicide. She did not tell her mom again, and she didn't tell her father until Philip died ten years later of alcohol-related problems. She was afraid her father would react violently or that he would blame her.

After Uncle Philip died, Alexandra finally revealed to her father what had happened. Sam immediately got his daughter the help she needed for emotional healing and tearfully asked Alexandra's forgiveness for not having protected her. In family therapy, her mother came to understand just how much she had hurt her daughter and acknowledged that she should have put her daughter's safety first.

Reflection Questions

1. How might Caroline have responded differently to her daughter, despite her conflicting family loyalties?

2. How would you respond if one of your children was ill at ease with an extended family member or family friend?

3. How might Sam and Caroline have set up a more protected family environment?

Manny's Diagnosis

Caroline didn't want to believe that her own brother was capable of sexual abuse, so her knee-jerk response was to blame the victim. And yet, by refusing to take her daughter's story seriously, Caroline compounded the damage to her daughter as well as her husband, who deserved to know what had happened to his daughter so he could protect her.

Once they became aware that their teenage daughter was uncomfortable around her uncle, both Sam and Caroline might have recognized that leaving the two of them home alone together was inappropriate and possibly dangerous. Protecting their daughter, rather than sparing the feelings of an extended family member, ought to have been their highest priority.

Form Your Children, Reform Yourselves

Parenting is a momentous task. It's like having your heart go walking around outside your body, as author Elizabeth Stone quipped. You aren't always in control of what happens to your children, particularly as they get older. But you can resolve to give them the best that you've got. And that often means setting a good example for them through your own behavior (CCC, 2223).

The best way to teach your children is to model the behavior you want them to imitate—and to reform yourself when necessary. No other professional occupation demands this. You can be a brilliant surgeon or lawyer but a horrible human being. You cannot be a good parent without being a good person. Sometimes children can even inspire you to improve your own life and become better than you are.

When we tell our children, "No dessert between meals," we remember that it's a healthy rule for us, too. When our young children sit next to us on the couch for TV time, we tend to avoid shows with bad language, excessive violence, or provocative love scenes. Many parents go back to church again or start a new habit of nighttime prayer for the sake of their children. Some parents start reading the Bible and *Catechism* or other spiritual books in order to prepare themselves to teach their son's or daughter's religious education class.

In order to form our children, we reform ourselves, and so our children teach us as we teach them. Or in the words of John Paul II, parents "communicate their own mature humanity to the newborn child, who gives them in turn the newness and freshness of the humanity which it has brought into the world" (*LF*, 16). And by handing down our faith-filled values to our children, we ensure that these values survive from generation to generation.

Bonus Material
Conversation Starters

- Thinking back to how your parents raised you, what would you like to imitate? What would you like to do differently?
- How do you plan to educate your children (public school, Catholic school, or homeschool)?
- Who are your favorite parent models—people whose approach to parenting you most admire and would most like to imitate?
- What are the biggest goals or dreams you have for your children?

Action Plan

Decide to spend special time having fun with each one of your children. Your spouse can watch the other kids while you take one of your children out to the park or for ice cream. If you don't have kids, offer to babysit for a niece or nephew.

Catechism Corner

"Parents have the first responsibility for the education of their children. They bear witness to this responsibility first by *creating a home* where tenderness, forgiveness,

respect, fidelity, and disinterested service are the rule"
(*CCC*, 2223).

11.

Turning Our Homes into Places of Prayer

THE ETERNAL CONSEQUENCES OF EVERYDAY FAMILY LIFE

> Only by praying together with their children can a father and mother—exercising their royal priesthood—penetrate the innermost depths of their children's hearts and leave an impression that the future . . . will not be able to efface.
> —Pope John Paul II, *Familiaris Consortio*, 60

When our son, Miguel, was about two years old, he would suddenly drop to his knees in prayer in completely unexpected places, like the middle of a public sidewalk. The whole family would wait a few moments for Miguel to finish and then we'd continue on our way. Manny and I melted at such cuteness. But we were also inspired by how prayer seemed as natural to our little boy as breathing. He showed us how our eternal and everlasting God is always ready to meet us in the here and now.

Prayer creates "a vital and personal relationship with the living and true God" (CCC, 2558). God thirsts for our love, just as we thirst to be loved (CCC, 2560). Prayer is like living water welling up in our hearts, drenching us in spiritual fulfillment (CCC, 2652). Few people think of prayer as "being in love with God and expressing that love in many diverse ways, often in touching and tender terms. But such is the scriptural reality" (*Prayer Primer* [*PP*], 35).

Honest, sincere prayer is not rote, superficial, or shallow. In the words of St. Thérèse of Lisieux, "Prayer is a surge of the heart" (quoted in CCC, 2558). Prayer helps us stir up our love for God and our charity for others, so that with the psalmist we can say, "My soul longs, indeed it faints for the courts of the LORD; my heart and my flesh sing for joy to the living God" (Ps 84:2).

When family members spend time together nurturing their friendship with God, they form a nearly unbreakable bond. In becoming closer to God, they become closer to each other. Evenings become filled with prayer instead of electronic entertainment, and Sundays become filled with praising God instead of hopping in separate minivans to drive different kids in different directions to various extracurricular activities. But commitment to family prayer can be difficult unless the parents first commit to strengthening their own prayer life.

Persevere in Prayer, Persevere in Love

If you're not used to praying every day or every week, getting started can be hard. It feels as if there's not enough time: the calendar is already too full; everyone is too stressed out and tired. It might even feel like a battle. But it's a battle worth fighting and worth winning, because it's a battle of love. "Against our dullness and laziness, the battle of prayer is that of humble, trusting, and persevering *love*" (CCC, 2742). The same battle is required to persevere in marriage and family life, and prayer is the ultimate weapon.

Family life naturally leads to prayer. "Births and birthday celebrations, wedding anniversaries of the parents, departures, separations and homecomings, important and far-reaching decisions, the death of those who are dear—all of those mark God's loving intervention in the family's history" (FC, 59). The events of ordinary life are constant reminders to thank God for his blessings and to seek his help in times of need or grief. Especially in times of severe crisis, prayer can keep marital communication alive and give hope for healing.

In Search of Everlasting Love

How Can Prayer Help Heal a Marriage?

Jim and Jennifer are in their fifties. This is the second marriage for each of them. Jim was raised to avoid confrontation and was reluctant to give up the sinful habits that had led to the breakdown of his first marriage. To avoid accountability for his behavior, he frequently made promises he couldn't keep or defended himself with a long litany of unconvincing excuses.

One of the issues that had created the greatest division in the marriage was Jim's use of pornography. His compulsive lies, broken promises, and constant cover-ups had seriously damaged their relationship. Because Jim had been raised only nominally Christian and Jennifer was a cradle

Catholic, they had very different ideas about sexuality. Jennifer believed that pornography was sinful. Jim thought watching porn was not that bad, just a private vice such as drinking or smoking. He perceived it as Jennifer's hang-up—her problem, not his.

In therapy, it became clear that Jim's porn habit was destroying their marriage. To overcome his addiction, Jim started attending Sexaholics Anonymous. But to heal the marriage, Jim and Jennifer were encouraged to begin praying together. A year later, Jim converted to Catholicism and obtained an annulment of his previous marriage so they could have their marriage blessed by the Church.

Reflection Questions

1. How might praying together help Jim be honest with Jennifer and with himself?

2. How might becoming Catholic strengthen Jim to overcome his addiction?

3. How might praying with her husband help Jennifer to forgive Jim?

Manny's Diagnosis

Prayer helped Jim and Jennifer reestablish healthy, honest intimate communication. Regular prayer made Jim accountable for his actions to God as well as to Jennifer. In the context of prayer, it was easier for Jim and Jennifer to listen to one another instead of launching into an argument. A shared prayer life helped Jennifer to show Christ's mercy and forgiveness to her husband. Through therapy, prayer, and attending the sacraments together, both of them stopped blaming each other and instead turned together to God to renew their marriage. After his conversion to Catholicism, Jim mostly overcame his struggles against porn, relapsing only in periods of great stress. It was an ongoing battle—and yet he now had the tools he needed to free himself from the chains of his addiction.

For our own happiness, the Bible urges us to pray always.[1] Prayer can bring peace to our hearts and our homes. Of course, "praying always" can be an intimidating goal—to begin, it's best to commit to pray at specific times (*CCC*, 2697). So the first step in cultivating a rich and nourishing prayer life is to schedule prayer time on the calendar, treating prayer like a meeting with an important client or best friend. Then you'll be less likely to "break the appointment."

There are many different ways to pray, so just pick your favorite (or find a new favorite) and get started. We'll make several suggestions later in the chapter, but beginners in the spiritual life often find it easiest to start with mental prayer.

Make Time to Pray for Yourself and Your Family

Mental prayer is a time set aside to speak to God in your own words. "This silent conversation is . . . the beginning stage of becoming more and more familiar with our unspeakable Creator dwelling in our soul" (*PP*, 68). Mental prayer fills you with the strength to confront the troubles of the day by providing a quiet time to recollect your thoughts and to ask God's help with whatever awaits you. Ten or fifteen minutes each day is not a large amount of time, and it can actually save time when you regularly commit to it. In mental prayer, you can set before God all the needs of yourself and your family, knowing that

praying for your family is one of the best things you can
do for them.

Prayer should be not only *for* your family but also
with your family. Going to Mass together on Sundays is a
ready-made way for a family to pray together. Holy Mass
is the source and summit of Christian life.[2] Worshipping
together as a community fills a deeply human need to
offer praise and adoration together. This communal worship in turn nourishes individual and family prayer. No
wonder the Church obligates Catholics to attend Holy
Mass every Sunday and on special feast days, called Holy
Days of Obligation (CCC, 2180).

Oma and Opa always took our family to church on
Sunday, even though as Episcopalians we had no obligation to go every week. Parishioners wanting to attend
services at R. E. Lee Episcopal Church (or "St. Bobby's" as
it was nicknamed) had only two choices: 8:00 a.m. or 10:30
a.m. Imagine my surprise when I learned that Catholic
churches near us offer Holy Mass once or twice on Saturday evenings and up to six times on Sunday! There are
family Masses, choir Masses, folk Masses, Latin Masses,
Spanish Masses, and even Masses in Polish or Portuguese.
Without question, at least in our area, there is a Mass for
everyone.

Every family member might not be equally enthused
about going to Mass, but that's okay. It's still important
to go together. When Manny and I started dating, he took
me to Mass every Sunday, and I wasn't even Catholic.
Many non-Catholic spouses go with their families for
Mass and just stay in the pew when it's time to receive
Holy Communion. Although children sometimes whine
and resist, combining Mass with a trip to Dunkin' Donuts
or Baskin-Robbins can convince even the most recalcitrant
child to go to Mass without too much complaint. Over
time they will learn that going to Mass is its own reward.

In Search of Everlasting Love

How Can Prayer Keep Families Connected, Even in Times of Crisis?

Frank and Maureen have been married eight years, and they have two kids, ages seven and five. When Frank had an affair with a woman from work, Maureen kicked him out of the house. According to Maureen, Frank was a good father but a lousy husband.

Although Frank and Maureen were both Catholics, they attended Mass only on Easter and Christmas, and prayer was not a big part of their life. Because Frank was eager to save his marriage, he stopped the extramarital affair and committed to doing the hard work he needed to do to reconcile with his family. He decided to cultivate a daily habit of prayer in order to receive the grace and strength he needed. With the help of a simple pamphlet, he was soon able to learn and pray all the mysteries of the Rosary.

Because he was physically separated from his family, praying the Rosary for his family helped to bridge this distance. He also began taking the kids to Mass every Sunday. Although Maureen didn't always go to Mass with them, Frank was still able to spend valuable time becoming closer to his kids and to God. And by alleviating some of the burden of childcare, Frank showed Maureen that he still cared about her needs, too.

Reflection Questions

1. How did crisis increase Frank's desire to pray?
2. How did prayer help Frank stay close to his family?

3. How did prayer help Maureen and the kids?

Manny's Diagnosis

Like many people, Frank did not feel the need to reach out to God until crisis hit. The good news is that God is always there to help us whenever we reach out. When Maureen kicked Frank out, he could no longer parent the kids through being physically present. But he remained spiritually present by praying for his family and did an even better job of spiritual fatherhood by starting a habit of taking the kids to weekly Mass. Frank's actions reinforced Maureen's belief that Frank was a good father and helped to relieve the difficulties of single motherhood that Maureen was experiencing.

Easy Prayer Habits for Families

While it isn't always easy to get the whole family together for an extended prayer time, the Church has a rich spiritual tradition, with many different ways to pray. Just as couples can start praying together in small ways to build up that intimate connection, so parents and children grow closer to each other as they grow closer to God.

One simple way to begin this practice of family prayer, in addition to Holy Mass, is morning and evening prayers and grace before meals (*CCC*, 2698; *FC*, 61). These prayers are quick, and since they're easy and fun for kids, they're a no-stress way for parents to fulfill their responsibility to introduce their children to God, so to speak, by educating their children in prayer (*FC*, 60).

Morning Prayer

Our family says its morning prayers in the car on the way to school. First, we sing the Gospel acclamation, or the "Alleluia," that the choir sang on our wedding day. The words were easy for the kids to learn, and the whole song takes no longer than a minute: "Alleluia, alleluia, alleluia. This is the day that the Lord has made. Let us rejoice and be glad. Alleluia, alleluia, alleluia." (You can use whatever tune the cantor at your parish sings before the Gospel reading at Sunday Mass.)

Then, each child says a few intentions. The kids usually pray for a good day at school and for us to have a good day at work or "doing whatever it is that Mom does." Our son, Miguel, likes to pray for the whole world and all the souls in purgatory. Sometimes he prays for his sisters not to take such a long time praying. It's fun to pick a different intention for every day of the week. Every Monday, we might pray for one particular family member, every Tuesday for another, and so on.

The whole process takes no longer than the five- or ten-minute ride to school. Our Spanish cousin Patricio got so used to our morning prayer ritual that he would start singing "alleluia" every time he sat down in our car.

Bedtime Prayers

Bedtime prayers can also provide a beautiful opportunity to share the faith with your children. Many parents love saying bedtime prayers with their children, particularly if they did the same thing with their own parents when they were little. The Church calls this evening prayer, and there are enough different kinds of evening prayer to please any family.

Oma taught me how to pray the Our Father at bedtime when I was young. We started with one line of the prayer and kept adding lines, night after night, until I learned all of it. Praying out loud together is vocal prayer (*CCC*, 2722).

Our children really enjoy praying for their friends and family at bedtime, which is a type of intercessory prayer (*CCC*, 2647). This is a wonderful way to communicate with your family and find out what really matters in their lives. Our friend Christina started asking her son to name his "consolations and desolations" at bedtime prayer when he got older. This just means the best and worst things that happened during the day. You can learn a lot about your children (and your spouse) this way.

As your children become old enough for their first confession, also known as First Penance, you can ask them to say how they experienced God's presence that day and help them to examine their conscience, a Catholic prayer tradition sometimes called the "examen" (*CCC*, 1454).

Lectio Divina

If you read your children a story at bedtime, you can choose a Bible story. A lot of Old Testament stories have as much action and adventure as any child could want. Prayerful reading of scripture is called lectio divina and has a long tradition in the Church (*CCC*, 1177). Daily devotional guides that suggest a Bible passage for every day are also a great way to learn what's in the Bible. You can customize your bedtime prayer ritual to whatever works best for your family.

Grace before Meals

Praying before meals can expose your children to the favorite prayers of both parents' families. Our family comes from many different faith traditions, and we try to honor them all in our mealtime prayers. Grace before breakfast begins with "God is great, God is good, and we thank him for our food . . ." The children learned this prayer in their parish school, and my father had also learned it as a child being brought up Methodist. Grace before lunchtime is the Patch Prayer (named for the family homestead), from my maternal grandfather's Pennsylvania Dutch roots: "We thank thee, Lord, so great and good, who doth provide our daily food. For all thy mercies rich and free, help us to show more love to thee. Amen." When my brother married a Jewish woman, we added the concluding line, "All the way with Yahweh!" At dinnertime, we recite the Spanish translation of the Catholic prayer, "Bless us, O Lord, and these, thy gifts, which we are about to receive."

Pray to Mary, Mother of Christ and of Christian Families

John Paul II also encouraged Catholic families to love and venerate the Blessed Virgin Mary, for "she who is the Mother of Christ and of the Church is in a special way the Mother of Christian families" (*FC*, 61). Either Manny or I will phone the other to pray the Marian prayer called the Angelus every day at noon. In the Angelus, we recite the scriptural passages about the angel Gabriel appearing to Mary to announce that she would give birth to the Messiah. It takes only a few minutes. Reciting the prayer together every day gives us a chance to reconnect in the middle of the day, and we often touch base on household matters, too.

When we're feeling especially brave, we attempt a family Rosary. The children know how to pray the Hail Mary, the Our Father, and the Glory Be at least by the time they are in kindergarten. Leading the Rosary can be fun for them, especially since some of the rosaries we have are quite special. One is made of crushed rose pet-als, bought in Rome, with a case displaying a picture of Pope Benedict XVI on one side and John Paul II on the other. Another one of our rosaries was blessed by a Chinese bishop who was imprisoned by his government for more than a decade. Yet another one has fifteen decades of beads, instead of the more traditional five.

While we pray the Rosary, we show the children beautiful representations in art of the mysteries they are supposed to be contemplating. When they were very little we rarely managed more than one decade, but it was a start. In October and May, we like to make family pilgrimages to nearby retreat houses and say the Rosary while walking around looking at different statues or shrines.

Our family has tried to develop a routine of special monthly and yearly times of prayer as well. On the first Friday of every month, Manny and I go out to dinner (our hot date night!) followed by adoration of the Blessed Eucharist, known as nocturnal vigil. This way, we reconnect with each other and with God. John Paul II pointed out a great need for this type of eucharistic worship. "Jesus awaits us in this sacrament of love. Let us not refuse the time to go meet him in adoration," he urged (quoted in CCC, 1380). It is especially beautiful for a husband and wife, joined by God, to share this sacrament of love together.

Once a year, Manny and I each make a silent guided retreat for three days, where we take the time to pray and learn, and contemplate God's will for us in the upcoming year. Manny prefers to make this retreat during Lent. Then, in late April, around the time of our wedding anniversary, he watches the kids over the weekend as his anniversary gift to me, so I can go on retreat, too.

Pray Always

These daily, weekly, monthly, and yearly rhythms of prayer lead quite naturally into a family atmosphere of almost continual prayer (see *CCC*, 2698). In this atmosphere, "praying without ceasing" seems not too difficult after all. Regular habits of prayer eventually lead to constant awareness, or mindfulness, of the presence of God. This mindfulness can be practiced at any time and is truly ceaseless prayer. As St. John Chrysostom explained, "It is possible to offer fervent prayer even while walking in public or strolling alone, or seated in your shop, . . . while buying or selling, . . . or even while cooking" (quoted in *CCC*, 2743). This awareness of God still leaves us free "to give unhindered attention to other people and to our work" (*PP*, 43–44). Knowing that God is there with us can help us to love others better and serve their needs with greater willingness.

A family whose life is filled with constant reminders of God can transform itself into a "'domestic Church' where God's children learn to pray . . . and to persevere in prayer" (*CCC*, 2685). At Baptism, each Christian receives the mission of a priest, prophet, and king. Married people fulfill this mission in the domestic Church of the family (*FC*, 50). When you pray with each other, teach your children to pray, and prepare them to receive the sacraments, you are exercising "the baptismal priesthood of the faithful . . . in the sacrament of marriage" (*FC*, 59). By making prayer a part of your everyday family life, you are setting a course for everlasting happiness.

Bonus Material

Conversation Starters

- Do you have a favorite prayer?

- Do you feel comfortable speaking to God in front of each other?
- What prayers would you most like your children to learn?
- Does your parish church appeal to you? Do other parishes in your area appeal to you more?

Action Plan

Talk to your spouse about what type of prayer speaks most to your heart. Commit to doing it regularly together, whether that's once a day or once a week—whatever works for you. Add prayer (or more prayer) to your bedtime routine with the kids, too. Don't wait. Get started tonight!

Catechism Corner

"Prayer is the life of the new heart. It ought to animate us at every moment. But we tend to forget him who is our life and our all. . . . We must remember God more often than we draw breath'" (*CCC*, 2697).

12.

Turning into a Happier, Holier Family

Jesus, Mary, and Joseph Can Show You How

> The Holy Family "will not fail to help Christian families—indeed, all the families in the world—to be faithful to their day-to-day duties, to bear the cares and tribulations of life, to be open and generous to the needs of others, and to fulfill with joy the plan of God in their regard."
> —Pope John Paul II, *Familiaris Consortio*, 86

The Holy Family of Jesus, Mary, and Joseph gives us the perfect example of how to live our married and family life to achieve happiness now on earth and eternally in heaven. God was the center of their lives—not sex, money, or even work. The Holy Family shows us that marriage is more than just the union of two people. Marriage is the union of two people with God through each other, loving each other in a way that is faithful, free, and fruitful—the

fruit of which goes on and on forever, blessing generations to follow.

Our friends Mike and Julie really loved the idea that
marriage is a kind of trinitarian union among husband,
wife, and God. So when Mike proposed to Julie around
Christmastime, he asked her, "Remember how you
always tell me it takes three to get married? Well, take a
look on the Christmas tree." Julie knew exactly where to
look because there was only one ornament of the Holy
Family on the tree. Hanging on the ornament was a beautiful engagement ring that Mike had designed himself
and had a jeweler custom-make especially for Julie. The
design of the ring was two semicircular white diamonds
on either side of a larger round yellow diamond, signify-
ing a husband and wife joined by Christ. That wonderful
marriage proposal and that exquisite ring symbolized for
Mike and Julie that just as Jesus was the center of the Holy
Family, Jesus would be the center of their marriage and
their family as well.

The Holy Family's influence is not limited to happy
couples, however. For those who have lost mothers,
fathers, or spouses through distance, divorce, or death,
the Holy Family has a special role to fill. Jesus gave Mary
to us as our mother, and her tenderness can make up for
any lack of feminine tenderness in our lives. He also gave
us Joseph as our fatherly protector and guide to com-
pensate for any masculine love missing from our lives.
Some men and women don't want to imitate their parents' marriages but don't know where to look for a better
model. The Holy Family can teach all of us, especially
the wounded, the broken, and the searching, how to persevere and triumph in the gargantuan task of pouring
ourselves out for our families.

The members of the Holy Family are not two-dimen-
sional characters from a fictional storybook. They existed

as real flesh and blood. Jesus was fully human and fully divine. Mary was fully human, although without original sin. Joseph, like us, was an ordinary person called to serve God by loving and caring for his family. The Holy Family was "a true human family, formed by the divine mystery" (*RC*, 21).

In the midst of this world-weary age, the Holy Family still has a treasured place in people's hearts.[1] Through their example, the Holy Family has inspired the formation of "countless other holy families" (*LF*, 23).

The right choice becomes clear to many people when they imagine what Jesus might have done in a similar situation. Faced with the quandaries of family life, married couples can also ask themselves what the Holy Family might have done.

Faithfulness through Joy and Sorrow

Like many couples, the Holy Family faced serious difficulties in their relationship. They confronted internal obstacles such as fear and external challenges such as "poverty, persecution and exile" (*FC*, 86). But through faith and love, they surmounted these obstacles.

The beginning of Joseph and Mary's relationship was marked by fear and uncertainty. When the angel Gabriel appeared to Mary in splendor and asked her to be the mother of the Messiah, she was greatly troubled and perplexed. She needed to hear the angel's reassuring words, "Do not be afraid" (Lk 1:30). When Joseph first learned that Mary was pregnant, he decided to divorce her quietly. Think of it—Joseph contemplating divorce! But then an angel appeared to Joseph in a dream and said, "Do not be afraid to take Mary as your wife" (Mt 1:18–20). When Joseph and Mary understood what God wanted, they accepted his plan wholeheartedly and immediately in spite of their fear.

Many couples, before and after the wedding, are nervous about the future. The future is frightening when you don't know whether it will bring good times or bad. In truth, it will bring both, because that's how life is this side of heaven. The remedy to fear is love—divine love, not just human love. "There is no fear in love, but perfect love casts out fear" (1 Jn 4:18).

When Joseph did as the angel commanded and took Mary into his home, his love for her was "given new birth by the Holy Spirit," who "molds every human love to perfection" (*RC*, 19). For all husbands and wives, the Holy Spirit can increase their love, "deepening within it everything of human worth and beauty" (*RC*, 19). Believing and trusting in God, we can accept the uncertainty of the future without being controlled by our fear.

Even though we can control our negative emotions, we still can't always control external circumstances, and neither could Joseph and Mary. The Holy Family had to pack up their household and flee in the middle of the night to Egypt to save their baby boy from King Herod's soldiers. In a place far away from home, Mary and Joseph struggled to build a new life for themselves without the support of close friends and family. When they returned to Nazareth, they had to live under the grinding heel of Roman oppression. Through it all, they remained united.

We all hope that times of trouble will unite us as spouses, but unfortunately the opposite often happens and a major crisis will tear a marriage apart. Mary and Joseph's unity stemmed from the presence of Jesus in their marriage.

Jesus was physically present in Mary and Joseph's marriage from the beginning, from the moment of his conception. Jesus is mysteriously present in our marriages because we are two gathered together in his name (*CCC*, 1613). But we can come closer to Jesus by receiving his

Real Presence, his real body and blood, in the Sacrament of the Eucharist. In this way, Jesus' presence can sustain our marriages, too.

Marriage is a great earthly sign of God's undying love for us, as revealed in the Bible. The Old Testament begins with the natural marriage of Adam and Eve, and the New Testament begins with the Jesus-centered marriage of Joseph and Mary (*RC*, 7). Finally, the New Testament ends, in the book of Revelation, with the marriage between Christ and his Church (Rv 21). In our journey as married couples, we are called to follow a similar path—beginning with a natural love like Adam and Eve's, with a devotion that is increased and deepened by the Sacrament of Matrimony, and then ending in Jesus' eternal embrace in heaven.

The marriage of Mary and Joseph was "the summit from which holiness spreads all over the earth" (*RC*, 7). Their marriage sanctified not only them but also the whole world, by being the setting for the coming of the Son of God in the flesh.

Unfortunately, we don't get to see how the Holy Family's witness affected those closest to them, such as their extended families. Jesus' grandparents never make an appearance in the Bible, and neither do his aunts and uncles. Early traditions of the Church tell us that Mary was probably an only child (*LS*, 309).

The Bible does portray a tender portrait of the relationship between Mary and her cousin Elizabeth, both of whom were pregnant at the same time. When Mary greeted Elizabeth, the baby in Elizabeth's womb "leaped for joy," and Elizabeth exclaimed, "Why has this happened to me, that the mother of my Lord comes to me?" (Lk 1:43–44). If Mary was the first Christian, so to speak, her cousin Elizabeth was quite possibly the second. Elizabeth's son became known as John the Baptist, who

announced the coming of Jesus as the Messiah and baptized him in the Jordan River (Mt 3). At least as far as
Elizabeth and John were concerned, salvation was a family affair.

Not all of Jesus' relatives joined his mission, however. In a scene verging on the hilarious, the Gospel of
Mark reports that after Jesus chose the twelve apostles,
his relatives "went out to restrain him, for people were
saying, 'He has gone out of his mind'" (3:21). Perhaps not
surprisingly under the circumstances, Jesus proclaimed a
few verses later, "Who are my mother and my brothers?
. . . Whoever does the will of God is my brother and sister
and mother" (3:33, 35).

We can comfort ourselves with the fact that even Jesus
had difficult relatives. But with the help of supportive relatives, such as John the Baptist, Jesus' message of Christianity has spread to every corner of the globe. Give God
thanks for the friends and family you have who support
your faith and your marriage, and don't be afraid to call
on them for help.

Free to Work, Free to Serve

God painted the Holy Family's mission in life with broad
strokes, leaving them free to fill in the details. Despite the
miraculous and prophetic circumstances of Jesus' conception, birth, and exile to a foreign land, for more than a
decade afterward the Holy Family dedicated themselves
to the basic tasks of survival. The years that Mary and
Joseph spent raising Jesus from a baby to a man who performed miracles were probably the most ordinary years in
their family life, very similar to our everyday experiences.
These hidden years, barely mentioned in the Bible, show
us how to find meaning, importance, and even holiness
in our daily lives.

The Holy Family lived far closer to the financial edge than modern workers, who generally have bank accounts, sick time, vacation time, and perhaps even retirement plans or pensions. As the late Fr. Benedict Groeschel, acclaimed author and speaker, said in one of his homilies, the Holy Family were peasants. They lived hand to mouth. Yet I can imagine every day being filled with love and laughter, peace and joy, and the certainty that they could depend on their own continuous hard work and God's providential care.

Although Jesus performed the miracle of loaves and fishes to feed thousands in his public life, he didn't make miracles every day to feed himself and his parents (see Mt 14:19–21; 15:34–38). He could have turned their water into wine or multiplied the food in the family pantry, but instead they all worked for it every day.

The Holy Family's work in the little home in Nazareth wasn't valuable because it resulted in masterpieces that we can still visit today in the world's great museums. It was valuable because work was how they served one another and showed their love for one another (*RC*, 22). Their ordinary married and family life had an extraordinary and supernatural dimension, just as ours can.

Mary's physical labor, like that of every mother tending to her family's needs, repeated in an endless cycle of "tireless devotion" (*Redemptoris Mater* [*RM*], 46). Clean clothes became dirty and needed laundering again, full bellies became empty and needed food again, and tidy rooms became messy and needed organizing again. Joseph and Jesus worked with their hands as carpenters, serving their neighbors' needs and probably fixing whatever needed fixing in their own house, just as many men do. If Jesus had performed daily miracles to feed his family, he would have missed out on an opportunity to serve and love in a very human way.

Like Jesus, Mary always had a humble heart of service and an eager willingness to help out. At the annunciation, the angel Gabriel told Mary not only that she would bear the Messiah but also that her cousin Elizabeth "in her old age has also conceived a son; and this is the sixth month for her who was said to be barren" (Lk 1:36). Despite the joyful news of her own pregnancy, Mary rushed into the hill country to help her cousin (see Lk 1:39–40), thinking first of others in need.

At the beginning of Jesus' public ministry, Mary again appeared in the role of helpmate. During the wedding at Cana, Mary noticed the simple domestic detail that the bride and groom had run out of wine. Perhaps Mary noticed because she had arrived early at the feast, before Jesus and his disciples, in order to help the bride and groom prepare (see Jn 2:1–2). That would explain why the servants obeyed her so readily when she directed them to do whatever her son told them (see 2:5).

In performing the miracle of turning water into wine at Mary's urging, Jesus was putting himself and his divine power at the service of others. Jesus' miracles were not self-aggrandizing publicity stunts. In the desert, the devil tempted Jesus to use his power to serve himself: to break his forty-day fast by turning stones into bread, to make a grand entrance by leaping off the pinnacle of the temple, or to rule the world and its kingdoms (see Mt 4:1–11). Jesus said no to these raw displays of power, but he said yes to his mother's quiet request to aid someone else.

From the hidden years to the public years, the Holy Family freely used their time, talents, and even divine power to help others and meet their needs. They trusted God and their own hard work to meet their own needs. Hard work and service to others is a path to holiness that's open to everyone. The Holy Family's cheerful willingness to put others first can sustain us in our struggles to do the same.

Precious Bodies

Many people wonder how Joseph and Mary could have had a real marriage, much less an ideal one, without having sex. Part of the confusion stems from the idea of marriage as socially sanctioned sex. But marriage is not all sex, all the time. Sex has a role to play in marriage, but it is not the whole of marriage.

The purpose of married sex is to unite the couple and to cooperate with God in bringing new life into the world (*CCC*, 2366). By completely committing themselves to following God's will, Mary and Joseph achieved total unity and immense supernatural fruitfulness. They didn't need the act of sex in order to fulfill either the unitive or the procreative purpose of marriage.

Mary and Joseph shared a deep spiritual intimacy greater than could ever be expected within the limits of human understanding (*RC*, 19). They had an indivisible union of souls and hearts (*RC*, 7). And their cooperation with God's plan for the birth of the Messiah brought new life to the world through God's direct intervention without the need for sex. Many husbands and wives feel that sex brings them closer together and renews the relationship, but Mary and Joseph's relationship couldn't possibly have been any closer.

They deeply appreciated each other's masculinity and femininity. Joseph's heart surely skipped a beat when he saw the lamplight glint off the softness of Mary's hair. Mary's heart must have overflowed with happiness when Joseph used his strength to protect and provide for their family during the day. But they cherished one another's bodies as temples of the Holy Spirit, and they chose to preserve each other's purity. "You were bought with a price," said St. Paul, referring to Jesus' death for our sakes, "therefore glorify God in your body" (1 Cor 6:20).

Mary and Joseph glorified God in their bodies through accepting the gift of their child. When Joseph took Mary into his home, he accepted her body already blooming with pregnancy. He accepted the body of the child Jesus growing in her. He accepted her incomparably exalted motherhood and his own fatherhood through their marriage bond (*RC*, 3, 7).

Mary and Joseph also glorified God in their bodies through the sacrifice of their sex life. When Joseph and Mary gave up sexual intimacy, they did it because sex matters *so much*, not because it matters too little. Sex matters because it's a gift of our body to another, and our bodies are gifts from God. Mary and Joseph gave their bodies totally to God in celibacy, a spousal love-offering to God himself, just as do priests and those in the religious life. Simply put, Mary and Joseph valued sex enough to give it up.

Even without sex, Mary and Joseph's love for one another was still spousal because it motivated them to make a total gift of self. Joseph placed all his life, work, virtues, and talents at the service of the Son of God and his mother (*RC*, 8). Mary was totally God's and totally Joseph's, because Joseph was totally God's (*RM*, 39; see *RC*, 7).

The Holy Family is like the Trinity, three united as one and sharing an endless love (see *CCC*, 2205). The Trinity is not complete without Father, Son, and Holy Spirit. The Holy Family was not complete without Jesus, and Jesus' humanity was not complete without the Holy Family. Jesus gave his entire self, including his body, to his family and to the whole human race when he took on flesh and became man. He gave us his body again by dying on the cross. Giving our body to another in total spousal love cannot be limited to sex.

Some people act as if heaven is a dim reflection of sex, but the truth is that sex is a dim reflection of heaven. God knows how great sex is. He made it! You think he can't outdo himself? Within the gates of heaven, the physical union of sex will be overshadowed by the more tender, exciting, joyful, and affirming spiritual union that convinces us beyond any doubt that we are loved and lovable, valued and valuable, and cherished beyond all reason.

Loving Totally through Parenting and Prayer

As all mothers and fathers know, parenting requires a total gift of love to the next generation. A baby, in its radical dependence, asks everything of its parents. But stop to think how difficult it is to be so helpless. And then imagine the God of the universe becoming a human being in its most vulnerable stage. When Jesus took flesh and became incarnate, he gave himself totally as a gift to all humanity.

Jesus chose to be born into a marriage and into a family. He could have chosen to descend down a ladder of angels' wings or to appear in a cloud of fire and glory. Instead, he began his mission on earth in the sheltering arms of a family, a tiny and seemingly insignificant baby bearing the seeds of greatness and entrusted with the salvation of the world.

Each one of us and each one of our children began as Jesus did, entering the world naked and helpless. But God, who knew us before we were born and knit our bones within the womb, is calling each of us to play our particular role in the history of salvation. That role includes taking care of our families with all the love in our hearts. And it will be enough.

Mary and Joseph embraced the simple duties of parenthood. Joseph attended the birth of the child Jesus, perhaps with no one else to help. After her baby was born,
Mary gently wrapped him in swaddling clothes and put
him to her breast (see Lk 2:6–7). She cuddled the baby
Jesus and kept him safe and warm. In his role as protector, Joseph kept his wife and child safe on the long and
difficult journey to Egypt. This is "the gospel of Jesus'
infancy" (RM, 20), and it has elements in common with
the story of every family and every child.

On the surface, Mary and Joseph were just ordinary
people from Nazareth (RC, 15). So they probably did what
ordinary parents do, taking care of their child's body,
mind, and soul. They helped their child to walk and to
talk. They taught him a trade. Perhaps they even taught
him how to read. We know that Jesus learned to read,
because he read aloud from the scriptures at the temple
as an adult (see Lk 4:16–17). Although Joseph and Mary
might not actually have taught their son to read, they
certainly made sure he learned. We do all these things
for our children, too.

But as Mary and Joseph went about their ordinary
parenting duties, extraordinary things were occurring.
While Mary nurtured her son's body and intellect, she
also nurtured his soul through her great faith (CCC, 506).
Mary was not just a biological parent. She and Joseph
were also the spiritual parents of Jesus, carefully tending
the garden of his soul (RM, 43–44).

Mary's motherhood included "the ability to combine
penetrating intuition with words of support and encouragement" (RM, 46). Every minute of the day could have
provided an opportunity to teach God the Son about God
the Father and how he wants us to live our lives.

If there was very little left in the larder after the
Roman tax collectors had come, perhaps Mary through

her tears had to teach Jesus how to go hungry, reminding him that "one does not live by bread alone, but by every word that comes from the mouth of the LORD" (Dt 8:3). These words of scripture, years later, helped Jesus to withstand the devil's temptation after being ravaged by forty days of hunger in the desert (see Mt 4:4). The lessons that parents teach their children can have impact far into adulthood.

Mary and Joseph also taught their son how to pray. As a child, Jesus learned from them "the words and rhythms of the prayer of his people" (*CCC*, 2599). And in a sense, Jesus taught his parents how to pray. Being in the presence of Jesus allowed Joseph and Mary to immerse themselves in constant contemplation of God. If prayer is essentially a "mysterious encounter" with God who is Love, then every minute of Joseph and Mary's family life was prayer (*CCC*, 2567).

The scenes we meditate on in the Rosary unfolded in real time and magnificent detail before the eyes of Jesus' parents. Each dramatic event presented an opportunity for prayer to pour forth from their souls. When new life was just beginning to grow in Mary's belly, she shared the good news with her cousin Elizabeth in a perfect prayer of thanksgiving and praise. "My soul magnifies the Lord," Mary exclaimed, "and my spirit rejoices in God my Savior" (Lk 1:46–47; *CCC*, 2619). At Jesus' birth, Joseph and Mary silently adored him together with the shepherds and Magi, paying homage to the King of Glory (see Lk 2:16–20; Mt 2:10–11; *CCC*, 2628). Our personal prayer can be given new life if we imagine how we would have felt in Mary and Joseph's place, seeing these things with our own eyes.

The Holy Family also participated in all the public rituals required for observant Jews of their time. Eight days after birth, Joseph had Jesus ritually circumcised (see Lk 2:21; *RC*, 11–12). Forty days after Jesus' birth, the Holy Family traveled to Jerusalem so the Blessed Mother could be ritually purified, although she was already pure (see Lk 2:22; *RC*, 13). Again to follow the religious law, Joseph and Mary made a pilgrimage to Jerusalem every Passover, taking Jesus with them when he turned twelve (see Lk 2:41–42).

St. Luke's gospel points out that they performed "everything required by the law of the Lord" (2:39). Although they could have considered themselves above the law, the Holy Family performed the required rituals because they believed in the value of public worship. No matter how close we feel to Jesus in our hearts, it's important for us to worship publicly together also.

But the supreme example of prayer given by the Holy Family happened at the annunciation and at the time of Christ's passion and death. Prayer is an invitation to an intimate relationship in which we give ourselves to God and he gives himself to us (*CCC*, 2558). Prayer is an acceptance of "thy will be done." When Mary said "let it be" and consented to be the mother of the Son of God, she surrendered herself to the divine will. When Jesus asked his Father to spare him from the horrible death of crucifixion and then said "yet, not my will but yours be done," he, too, surrendered himself, body and soul, in complete faith, hope, trust, and love (Lk 22:42).

Mary and Jesus offered their whole beings in communion with God in an act of perfect prayer. They show us through their passionate deeds that the most sublime end of Christian prayer is "to be wholly God's, because he is wholly ours" (*CCC*, 2617). And their total gift of self had eternal consequences.

When Jesus took on flesh and then sacrificed his body on the cross for our salvation, he opened the gates of heaven and put eternity within the reach of every human being. When Mary and Joseph welcomed love into their family, in the form of a little child, they changed the world and made possible the world to come. If we give ourselves totally to our marriages, treating them as paths to heaven for ourselves and our children, we, too, can find joy forever.

Our God is very near to us (see Dt 4:7). Jesus not only gave himself to us on the cross and in the Sacrament of the Eucharist but also left us his teachings and example to follow. He established his Church to guide us with its wisdom (CCC, 763, 766), and he gave us Mary and Joseph to show us how to be good mothers and fathers, husbands and wives. ßWe hope these gifts of God's love and wisdom will help you on your journey as much as they have helped us.

God has handed you the keys to everlasting love: how to love faithfully, freely, fruitfully, and totally, both now and forever. Unlock the door and step through.

Bonus Material

Conversation Starters

- Do you see any similarities between your life and the Holy Family's?
- How easy is it to make God the center of your family life?
- What pulls you away from God the most?
- What unites you most as a couple? As a family? Can you become more united?

Action Plan

Pick one scene from the gospels about the life of the Holy Family. Meditate on how God speaks to you through their life and example. Make it a goal to imitate one of their virtues over the next year in order to improve your marriage.

Catechism Corner

"Christ chose to be born and grow up in the bosom of the holy family of Joseph and Mary. The Church is nothing other than 'the family of God'" (CCC, 1655).

Acknowledgments

Our special thanks are due to the following people:

- our editors, Heidi Hess Saxton and Bob Hamma, for answering all questions large or small and guiding our way with wisdom and grace;
- our family and friends for their stories, prayers, and good examples; and
- our beta readers, Opa, José, Sarah Reinhard, Ellen Gable Hrkach, James B., Prof. Michael Hoonhout, Deacon Scott Dodge, and Nona Aguilar.

Appendix A

How to Use This Book with a Group

ESPECIALLY FOR GROUP LEADERS AND CATECHISTS

We designed this book to be used in either four or twelve sessions. You can read one part a month or one chapter a week. Whether each session lasts one hour or two is up to you.

If you'd like your parish to use this book, working within existing structures is best. That way, no one has to reinvent the wheel. The book could replace or supplement written materials currently used for marriage preparation, marriage enrichment, adult faith formation, and catechist or deacon training programs.

Getting a group of friends together at your home to share everyone's thoughts about the book can also really enhance your reading experience. If you already belong to a home-based book club or prayer circle, your organizational work is done. Just suggest or recommend the book at your regular meetings. If you don't already belong to a group like that, you can set up your own. It's an opportunity to deepen the friendships you have and to make new ones with married couples who are on the same journey.

The timing of the group depends upon who's in it. If your group is mostly engaged or newlywed couples with no kids, you might want to meet on a weekend night; bring beer, wine, and snacks and make a party out of it.

If your friends are old enough to have kids, you might want to pick a Sunday afternoon and provide free on-site babysitting. If you don't know any grandmothers or teenagers willing to volunteer (maybe for Confirmation service hours), some of the parents might want to chip in a few dollars each to split the cost between them.

Stay-at-home moms can meet during the school day and discuss the book with their husbands afterward. People with jam-packed schedules might want the flexibility of a Facebook group or Google+ community, whose moderator announces the chapter and topic for the week and invites everyone to comment whenever they have the chance.

If you're starting a new group, try to gather at least three core members dedicated to making it happen. Each core member can suggest names of ten individuals or couples who might want to join. Even if half of the people invited don't come, you'll still have a good-sized group. Make sure you get everyone's e-mail addresses and phone numbers so you can remind them before each session.

The three core members can also share the responsibility for leading the discussion. The discussion leader can summarize the chapter or chapters and ask people for their general reactions. Then the leader can guide the group through the end-of-chapter questions.

If the leader takes the first stab at answering the questions, it may encourage the other participants to share. Although it's best to ask participants to read the relevant part of the book before the meeting, the questions are open ended and even folks who didn't get a chance to review the material ahead of time can talk about how issues such as sex, money, and child rearing affect their marriage.

Last but not least, don't forget to begin and end with a prayer. You can say the Hail Mary, the Come Holy Spirit, or any other prayer that's most meaningful to the group. If you ask for the Holy Family's intercession and guidance, you won't be disappointed.

> Jesus, Mary, and Joseph, Holy Family of Nazareth, pray for us!

Appendix B

More Resources to Explore

Chapter 1:
Turning Two into One

Books

Calis, Stephanie. *Invited: The Ultimate Catholic Wedding Planner*. Boston: Pauline Books and Media, 2016.

Popcak, Greg, and Lisa Popcak. *Just Married: The Catholic Guide to Surviving and Thriving in the First Five Years of Marriage*. Notre Dame, IN: Ave Maria Press, 2013.

Roback Morse, Jennifer, and Betsy Kerekes. *101 Tips for a Happier Marriage: Simple Ways for Couples to Grow Closer to God and to Each Other*. Notre Dame, IN: Ave Maria Press, 2013.

Tomeo (Pastore), Teresa, and Dominick Pastore. *Intimate Graces: How Practicing the Works of Mercy Brings Out the Best in Marriage*. Notre Dame, IN: Ave Maria Press, 2015.

Waiss, John R. *Couples in Love: Straight Talk on Dating, Respect, Commitment, Marriage, and Sexuality*. New York: The Crossroad Publishing Company, 2003.

Videos and Internet Resources

For Your Marriage. Online initiative of the US Conference of Catholic Bishops. http://www.foryourmarriage.org.

Santos, Karee. *Can We Cana? A Community to Support Catholic Marriages* (blog). http://canwecana.blogspot.com.

Together for Life Online. Outreach of Ave Maria Press. http://www.togetherforlifeonline.com.

When Two Become One. DVD. Rockville Centre, NY: Diocese of Rockville Centre, Office of Faith Formation, 2008. Available for purchase at http://drvc-faith.mybigcommerce.com.

Chapter 2:
Turning Good Marriages into Pathways to Glory

Books

Hahn, Scott. *First Comes Love: Finding Your Family in the Church and the Trinity.* New York: Doubleday, 2002.

Hildebrand, Dietrich von. *Marriage: The Mystery of Faithful Love.* Manchester, NH: Sophia Institute Press, 1991.

Holböck, Ferdinand. *Married Saints and Blesseds through the Centuries.* San Francisco: Ignatius Press, 2002.

May, William. *Marriage: The Rock on Which the Family Is Built.* 2nd ed. San Francisco: Ignatius Press, 2009.

Sheen, Fulton J. *Three to Get Married.* Princeton, NJ: Scepter Publishers, 1996.

Videos and Internet Resources

US Conference of Catholic Bishops. *Marriage: Love and Life in the Divine Plan.* Pastoral letter. Washington, DC: Author, 2009. Available free at http://www.usccb.org.

———. "Saying I Do: What Happens at a Catholic Wedding." Free video resource. Accessed August 25, 2015. http://www.usccb.org.

Chapter 3:
Turning Union into Communion

Books

Bennett, Art, and Laraine Bennett. *The Temperament God Gave Your Spouse*. Manchester, NH: Sophia Institute Press, 2008.

DeArmond, Deb. *Related by Chance, Family by Choice: Transforming Mother-in-Law and Daughter-in-Law Relationships*. Grand Rapids, MI: Kregel Publications, 2013.

Donoghue, Paul J., and Mary E. Siegel. *We Really Need to Talk: Steps to Better Communication*. Notre Dame, IN: Sorin Books, 2010.

Guarendi, Ray. *Marriage: Small Steps, Big Rewards*. Cincinnati: Servant Books, 2011.

MacNutt, Francis. *The Prayer That Heals: Praying for Healing in the Family*. Rev. ed. Notre Dame, IN: Ave Maria Press, 2005.

Popcak, Gregory K. *God Help Me! These People Are Driving Me Nuts! Making Peace with Difficult People*. 2nd ed. New York: The Crossroad Publishing Company, 2010.

Internet Resources

Fitzgibbons, Richard P. Institute for Marital Healing. http://www.maritalhealing.com.

Chapter 4:
Turning Meaningless Drudgery into Meaningful Work

Books

Durand, Dave. *Time Management for Catholics: Make the Most of Every Second by Putting Christ First*. New York: The Crossroad Publishing Company, 2012.

Hain, Randy. *The Catholic Briefcase: Tools for Integrating Faith and Work*. Liguori, MO: Liguori Publications, 2011.

Martin, Stephen. *The Messy Quest for Meaning: Five Catholic Practices for Finding Your Vocation*. Notre Dame, IN: Sorin Books, 2012.

Pierce, Gregory F. A. *Spirituality at Work: 10 Ways to Balance Your Life On the Job*. Chicago: Loyola Press, 2001.

Thompson, William David. *On-the-Job Prayers: 101 Reflections and Prayers for Christians in Every Occupation*. Skokie, IL: ACTA Publications, 2006.

Internet Resources

Catholic Women's Guide. *Setting the World on Fire Blog: Biz and Life Tips for Catholic Women Entrepreneurs*. http://www.catholicwomensguide.com.

The Integrated Catholic Life: Helping You to Integrate Faith, Family and Work. http://www.integrated catholiclife.org.

Chapter 5:
Turning Ownership into Stewardship

Books

Dayton, Howard, Jon Bean, and Evelyn Bean. *Your Money Counts*. Catholic ed. Chermside, Australia: Compass Catholic Ministries, 2013.

Lenahan, Phil. *Seven Steps to Becoming Financially Free: A Catholic Guide to Managing Your Money.* Huntington, IN: Our Sunday Visitor, 2006.

Nichols, Dwight. *God's Plans for Your Finances.* New Kensington, PA: Whitaker House, 1998.

Internet Resources

Lenahan, Phil. Veritas Financial Ministries. http://www.veritasfinancialministries.com.

The National Marriage Project. "The State of Our Unions: Marriage in America 2009; Money and Marriage." December 2009. http://stateofourunions.org.

US Conference of Catholic Bishops. *Stewardship: A Disciple's Response.* 10th anniversary ed. Washington, DC: Author, 2012. Ebook available at Amazon and iTunes.

Chapter 6:
Turning Inaction into Action

Books

Doyle Roche, Mary M. *Schools of Solidarity: Families and Catholic Social Teaching.* Collegeville, MN: Liturgical Press, 2015.

McKenna, Kevin E. *A Concise Guide to Catholic Social Teaching.* Notre Dame, IN: Ave Maria Press, 2002.

Francis. *The Church of Mercy: A Vision for the Church.* Chicago: Loyola Press, 2014.

Pontifical Council for Justice and Peace. *Compendium of the Social Doctrine of the Church.* Vatican City: Libreria Editrice Vaticana, 2004.

Weber, Kerry. *Mercy in the City: How to Feed the Hungry, Give Drink to the Thirsty, Visit the Imprisoned, and Keep Your Day Job.* Chicago: Loyola Press, 2014.

Wright, Paul A. *Mother Teresa's Prescription: Finding Happiness and Peace in Service.* Notre Dame, IN: Ave Maria Press, 2006.

Internet Resources

US Conference of Catholic Bishops. "Catholic Social Teaching." Accessed August 26, 2015. http://www.usccb.org.

————. "A Place at the Table: A Catholic Recommitment to Overcome Poverty and to Respect the Dignity of All God's Children; A Pastoral Reflection of the US Catholic Bishops." November 13, 2002. http://www.usccb.org.

Chapter 7:
Turning Spouses into Life-Giving Lovers

Books

Eden, Dawn. *The Thrill of the Chaste: Finding Fulfillment while Keeping Your Clothes On.* Catholic ed. Notre Dame, IN: Ave Maria Press, 2015.

Hahn, Kimberly. *Life-Giving Love: Embracing God's Beautiful Design for Marriage.* Ann Arbor, MI: Charis, 2001.

Healy, Mary. *Men and Women Are from Eden: A Study Guide to John Paul II's Theology of the Body.* Cincinnati: Servant Books, 2005.

Popcak, Gregory K. *Holy Sex! A Catholic Guide to Toe-Curling, Mind-Blowing, Infallible Loving.* New York: The Crossroad Publishing Company, 2008.

Spinello, Richard A. *Understanding Love and Responsibility: A Companion to Karol Wojtyla's Classic Work.* Boston: Pauline Books and Media, 2014.

West, Christopher. *Good News about Sex and Marriage*. Rev. ed. Cincinnati: Servant Books, 2004.

Internet Resources

Catholic Answers. "What Is Chastity?" http://www.chastity.com.

Chapter 8:
Turning the Fear of Fertility into a Total Gift of Self

Books

Aguilar, Nona. *The New No-Pill, No-Risk Birth Control*. New York: Rawson Associates, 1986.

Bachiochi, Erika, ed. *Women, Sex, and the Church: A Case for Catholic Teaching*. Boston: Pauline Books and Media, 2010.

Coffin, Patrick. *Sex au Naturel: What It Is and Why It's Good for Your Marriage*. Steubenville, OH: Emmaus Road Publishing, 2010.

Fisher, Simcha. *The Sinner's Guide to Natural Family Planning*. Huntington, IN: Our Sunday Visitor, 2014.

Franks, Angela. *Contraception and Catholicism: What the Church Teaches and Why*. Boston: Pauline Books and Media, 2013.

Hilgers, Thomas W. *The NaPro Technology Revolution: Unleashing the Power in a Woman's Cycle*. New York: Beaufort Books, 2010.

Kippley, Sheila Matgen. *Breastfeeding and Natural Child Spacing: How Ecological Breastfeeding Spaces Babies*. Cincinnati: Couple to Couple League, 1999.

Ruhi-López, Angelique, and Carmen Santamaría. *The Infertility Companion for Catholics: Spiritual and Practical*

Support for Couples. Notre Dame, IN: Ave Maria Press, 2012.

Weschler, Toni. *Taking Charge of Your Fertility: The Definitive Guide to Natural Birth Control, Pregnancy Achievement, and Reproductive Health.* 20th anniversary ed. New York: William Morrow Paperbacks, 2015.

Internet Resources

IuseNFP. http://www.iusenfp.com. Includes a useful quiz to determine which method is best for you.

Living the Sacrament: A Catholic NFP Community. http://www.livingthesacrament.com.

US Conference of Catholic Bishops. "Married Love and the Gift of Life." November 2006. http://www.usccb .org.

Chapter 9:
Turning Challenges into Channels of Grace

Books

Hain, Randy. *Special Children, Blessed Fathers: Encouragement for Fathers of Children with Special Needs.* Steubenville, OH: Emmaus Road, 2015.

Rizzo, David. *Faith, Family, and Children with Special Needs: How Catholic Parents and Their Kids with Special Needs Can Develop a Richer Spiritual Life.* Chicago: Loyola Press, 2012.

Thomas, Theresa, and Patti Armstrong, eds. *Big Hearted: Inspiring Stories from Everyday Families.* New Rochelle, NY: Scepter Publishers, 2013 (about big families).

Wolfe, Jaymie Stuart. *Adoption: Room for One More?* Boston: Pauline Books and Media, 2015.

Internet Resources

Be Not Afraid: Peer-Based Support to Parents Experiencing a Prenatal Diagnosis and Carrying to Term. http://www.benotafraid.net.

Hendey, Lisa. "Resources for Catholic Step Parents and Blended Families." CatholicMom.com. Accessed August 26, 2015. http://catholicmom.com.

Saxton, Heidi Hess. "The Blogroll: Helpful Sites for Families with Struggling Kids." *A Mother on the Road Less Traveled* (blog). July 11, 2009. https://heidihesssaxton.wordpress.com (includes fostering resources).

Chapter 10:
Turning Children into Adults

Books

Guarendi, Ray. *Discipline That Lasts a Lifetime: The Best Gift You Can Give Your Kids.* Ann Arbor, MI: Servant Books, 2003.

Lloyd, Susie. *Yes, God! What Ordinary Families Can Learn about Parenting from Today's Vocation Stories.* Notre Dame, IN: Ave Maria Press, 2013.

Meeker, Meg. *Strong Fathers, Strong Daughters: 10 Secrets Every Father Should Know.* New York: Ballantine Books, 2007.

———. *Strong Mothers, Strong Sons: Lessons Mothers Need to Raise Extraordinary Men.* New York: Ballantine Books, 2015.

Muldoon, Tim, and Sue Muldoon. *Six Sacred Rules for Families: A Spirituality for the Home*. Notre Dame, IN: Ave Maria Press, 2013.

Popcak, Gregory K., and Lisa Popcak. *Parenting with Grace: The Catholic Parents' Guide to Raising Almost Perfect Kids*. 2nd ed. Huntington, IN: Our Sunday Visitor, 2010.

Stenson, James B. *Compass: A Handbook on Parent Leadership*. New York: Scepter Publishers, 2003.

Internet Resources

Catholic Education Resource Center (CERC). "Parenting" (resources). Accessed August 26, 2015. http://www.catholiceducation.org.

Chapter 11:
Turning Our Homes into Places of Prayer

Books

Anderson, Christopher, Susan Gleason Anderson, and LaVonne Neff, eds. *A Prayer Book for Catholic Families*. Chicago: Loyola Press, 2008.

Clayton, David, and Leila Marie Lawler. *The Little Oratory: A Beginner's Guide to Praying in the Home*. Manchester, NH: Sophia Institute Press, 2014.

Collins, Christopher S. *Three Moments of the Day: Praying with the Heart of Jesus*. Notre Dame, IN: Ave Maria Press, 2014.

Francis. *Praying the Rosary with Pope Francis*. Edited by US Conference of Catholic Bishops. Washington, DC: Libreria Editrice Vaticana, 2014.

John Paul II. *Rosarium Virginis Mariae (On the Most Holy Rosary)*. Apostolic exhortation. Boston: Pauline Books and Media, 2002.

Mazza Urbanski, Grace. *Pray with Me: Seven Simple Ways to Pray with Your Children*. Notre Dame, IN: Ave Maria Press, 2015.

Muldoon, Tim, and Sue Muldoon. *Six Sacred Rules for Families: A Spirituality for the Home*. Notre Dame, IN: Ave Maria Press, 2013.

Videos and Internet Resources

Aycka Soft. Laudate. Free Catholic prayer app for smartphones. Available through Google Play and iTunes.

Toups, Mark. *Oremus: A Guide to Catholic Prayer*. West Chester, PA: Ascension Press, 2013. Available in DVD, Audio CD, paperback, and workbook format.

Universalis. Website providing the psalms and prayers for the Liturgy of the Hours. http://www.universalis.com.

Chapter 12:
Turning into a Happier, Holier Family

Books

Bossert, Denise. *Gifts of the Visitation: Nine Spiritual Encounters with Mary and Elizabeth*. Notre Dame, IN: Ave Maria Press, 2015.

Calloway, Donald. *Mary of Nazareth: The Life of Our Lady in Pictures*. San Francisco: Ignatius Press, 2014.

Fenelon, Marge. *Our Lady, Undoer of Knots: A Living Novena*. Notre Dame, IN: Ave Maria Press, 2015.

Miravalle, Mark. *Meet Your Mother: A Brief Introduction to Mary*. Rev. ed. Stockbridge, MA: Marian Press, 2014.

————. *Meet Your Spiritual Father: A Brief Introduction to St. Joseph*. Stockbridge, MA: Marian Press, 2015.

Pope Benedict XVI. *Jesus of Nazareth: From the Baptism in the Jordan to the Transfiguration*. New York: Doubleday, 2007.

Sheed, F. J. *To Know Christ Jesus*. Illus. ed. Tacoma, WA: Angelico Press, 2013.

Sheen, Fulton J. *The World's First Love: Mary, Mother of God*. 2nd ed. San Francisco: Ignatius Press, 2010.

Sri, Edward. *Walking with Mary: A Biblical Journey from Nazareth to the Cross*. New York: Image, 2013.

Notes

Introduction

1. Pontifical Council for the Family, *Preparation for the Sacrament of Marriage* (Boston: Pauline Books and Media, 1996), no. 10.

2. Ibid., nos. 3, 35, 36, 46, 56, 58, 66.

1. Turning Two into One

1. John M. Gottman, PhD, and Nan Silver, *The Seven Principles for Making Marriage Work: A Practical Guide from the Country's Foremost Relationship Expert*, 2nd ed. (New York: Random House, 2015), 138–139.

2. Public Religion Research Institute, "Fact Sheet: American Catholics and Public Policy," March 21, 2014, http://publicreligion.org.

3. Josemaría Escrivá de Balaguer, *Christ Is Passing By: Homilies* (New York: Scepter Publishers, 2002), no. 43.

2. Turning Good Marriages into Pathways to Glory

1. Fr. John Laux, M.A., *Mass and the Sacraments* (Rockford, IL: TAN Books, 1990), 87.

2. Javier Abad and Eugenio Fenoy, *Marriage: A Path to Sanctity*, 2nd ed. (Manila, Philippines: Sinag-Tala Publishers, 2002), 33.

3. Tertullian, *Ad uxorem*, 2, 8, 6–7: PL 1, 1412–1413, quoted in *CCC*, 1642.

4. John Paul II, *The Meaning of Vocation in the Words of John Paul II* (Princeton, NJ: Scepter Publishers, 1997), 28.

4. Turning Meaningless Drudgery into Meaningful Work

1. Balaguer, *Christ Is Passing By*, no. 47

2. John Paul II, *Meaning of Vocation*, 26.

3. Gianna Beretta Molla, *Love Letters to My Husband*, ed. Elio Guerriero (Boston: Pauline Books and Media, 2002), 10–15.

4. John Paul II, *Letter to Women*, 2, http://vatican.va.

5. John Paul II, *Meaning of Vocation*, 26.

6. Josemaría Escrivá de Balagner, *Furrow* (New York: Scepter Publishers, 1992), no. 300; Lv 22:20.

7. Jennifer Fulwiler, "It's Not What You Do, It's Whom You Serve," *Conversion Diary* (blog), September 25, 2008, http://jenniferfulwiler.com/.

5. Turning Ownership into Stewardship

1. "Homily of Pope John Paul II during the Holy Mass at the Capitol Mall in Washington, DC," October 7, 1979.

2. "Even the decision to invest in one place rather than another, in one productive sector rather than another, is always *a moral and cultural choice*." John Paul II, *Centesimus Annus* (1991), no. 36.

3. Phil Lenahan, *Seven Steps to Becoming Financially Free: A Catholic Guide to Managing Your Money* (Huntington, IN: Our Sunday Visitor, 2006), 77.

4. John Chrysostom, *On Living Simply: The Golden Voice of John Chrysostom*, comp. Robert Van de Weyer (Liguori, MO: Triumph Books, 1997), 7.

5. Pontifical Council for Justice and Peace, *Compendium of the Social Doctrine of the Church* (Vatican City: Libreria Editrice Vaticana, 2004), no. 355.

6. US Census Bureau, "Poverty: 2014 Highlights," accessed August 21, 2015, http://www.census.gov.

6. Turning Inaction into Action

1. Pope Francis, *Lumen Fidei* (Boston: Pauline Books and Media, 2013), no. 27.

7. Turning Spouses into Life-Giving Lovers

1. Linda J. Waite and Maggie Gallagher, *The Case for Marriage: Why Married People Are Happier, Healthier, and Better Off Financially* (New York: Broadway Books, 2001), 79.

2. Kimberly Hahn, *Life-Giving Love: Embracing God's Beautiful Design for Marriage* (Ann Arbor, MI: Charis, 2001), 113.

3. Ibid.

4. Paul S. Loverde, "Bought with a Price: Pornography and the Attack on the Living Temple of God," Catholic Diocese of Arlington, November 30, 2006, http://www.arlingtondiocese .org/.

5. Galena K. Rhoades and Scott M. Stanley, "Before 'I Do': What Do Premarital Experiences Have to Do with Marital Quality among Today's Young Adults?" National Marriage Project, University of Virginia, 2014, 6.

6. Cardinal Joseph Mindszenty, "Mother Card," accessed Sept. 7, 2015, http://www.mindszenty.org/Mother_father .aspx

8. Turning the Fear of Fertility into a Total Gift of Self

1. Richard J. Fehring, "Under the Microscope: The Facts about Faithful Catholics and Contraception," NFPP/US Conference of Catholic Bishops, Washington, DC, *Current Medical Research* 23, nos. 1 and 2 (Winter/Spring 2012): 16.

2. Ibid., 17.

3. Kimberly Daniels, William D. Mosher, and Jo Jones, "Contraceptive Methods Women Have Ever Used: United States 1982–2010," Centers for Disease Control and Prevention, *National Health Statistics Reports*, no. 62 (February 14, 2013): 13, table 4; Ada Slivinski, "Women spurning the pill for non-religious reasons," *Vancouver 24 Hrs*, May 13, 2014, http://van couver.24hrs.ca.

4. Christopher West, *Good News about Sex and Marriage: Answers to Your Honest Questions about Catholic Teaching*, rev.

ed. (Cincinnati: Servant Books, 2004), 127; John Wilks, "The Pill—How It Works and Fails," Oct. 1998, http://www.pfli.org.

5. Guttmacher Institute, "Fact Sheet: Induced Abortion in the United States," July 2014, http://www.guttmacher.org.

6. Stephen R. Pallone and George R. Bergus, "Fertility Awareness–Based Methods: Another Option for Family Planning," *Journal of the American Board of Family Medicine* 22, no. 2 (March–April 2009): 150.

7. Daniels, Mosher, and Jones, "Contraceptive Methods," 6–8, fig. 2.

8. Pallone and Bergus, "Fertility Awareness–Based Methods," 148–149, tables 1 and 2.

9. Ibid., 150–151.

10. St. Augustine, *Enarrat. in Ps. 143*, quoted in Pope Pius XI, *Casti Connubii (On Christian Marriage)* (1930), no. 98.

11. Centers for Disease Control and Prevention (CDC), American Society for Reproductive Medicine, and Society for Assisted Reproductive Technology, *2012 Assisted Reproductive Technology: National Summary Report* (Atlanta: US Department of Health and Human Services, 2014), 3, 14.

12. Richard J. Fehring, "Fertility/Infertility: Retrospective Cohort Efficacy Study of Natural Procreative Interventions to Treat Infertility," NFPP/US Conference of Catholic Bishops, Washington, DC, *Current Medical Research* 20, nos. 1 and 2 (Winter/Spring 2009): 6.

9. Turning Challenges into Channels of Grace

1. Elizabeth Matthews, *Precious Treasure: The Story of Patrick* (Steubenville, OH: Emmaus Road Publishing, 2002), 35.

2. Kent Gilges, *A Grace Given: A Father's Love for a Dying Child* (New Rochelle, NY: Scepter Publishers, 2012).

3. Bruce Barket and Mary Kay Barket, "Opinion: How Our Maggie Transforms Our Lives," *Newsday*, September 14, 2014, http://www.newsday.com.

4. John Paul II, *Dominum et vivificantem* (Washington, DC: US Catholic Conference, 1986), no. 10.

5. Timothy P. O'Malley, "A Trinitarian Love," *America*, September 23, 2013, http://americamagazine.org/issue/trinitarian-love.

10. *Turning Children into Adults*

1. "Canon 1136," reprinted in John P. Beal, James A. Coriden, and Thomas J. Green, eds., *New Commentary on the Code of Canon Law* (Mahwah, NJ: Paulist Press, 2000): 1357.

2. National Center for Learning Disabilities, *The State of Learning Disabilities*, 3rd ed. (New York: National Center for Learning Disabilities 2014), http://www.ncld.org/WP-content/uploads/2014/11/2014-State-of-LD.pdf; Centers for Disease Control and Prevention, "Attention-Deficit/Hyperactivity Disorder (ADHD): Data and Statistics," last updated July 8, 2015, http://www.cdc.gov/ncbddd/adhd/data.html; Centers for Disease Control and Prevention, "Autism Spectrum Disorder (ASD): Facts about ASD," last updated February 24, 2015, http://www.cdc.gov/ncbddd/autism/facts.html.

3. "More's Letter to His Children's Tutor, William Gunnell," May 22, 1518, The Center for Thomas More Studies, accessed August 24, 2015, http://www.thomasmorestudies.org.

4. Saint Francis de Sales, *Introduction to the Devout Life* (New York: Vintage Books, 2002), 147.

5. Children's Bureau (Administration for Children and Families) of the US Department of Health and Human Services, "Child Maltreatment 2012," December 17, 2013, x–xi, 21–22, 46, http://www.acf.hhs.gov.

6. US Conference of Catholic Bishops, *Walk in the Light: A Pastoral Response to Child Sexual Abuse* (Washington, DC: US Catholic Conference, 1995), http://www.usccb.org.

7. Ibid.

11. Turning Our Homes into Places of Prayer

1. CCC, 2742; Ps 1:1–2; 1 Thes 5:17–18; Eph 5:18–20; Eph 6:18.

2. Second Vatican Ecumenical Council, *Lumen Gentium (Dogmatic Constitution on the Church)*, November 21, 1964, no. 11.

12. Turning into a Happier, Holier Family

1. Synod of Bishops, *Instrumentum Laboris (The Vocation and Mission of the Family in the Church and the Contemporary World): The Pastoral Challenges of the Family in the Context of Evangelization*, June 26, 2014, no. 36.

Karee Santos is a Catholic blogger and speaker and a writer for the Catholic Match Institute. She has written numerous articles on marriage and family for the *National Catholic Register, Catholic Digest, Faith & Family* magazine, CatholicLane.com, AmazingCatechists.com, and Aleteia .org. She blogs at *Can We Cana?*

Manuel Santos, MD, is a psychiatrist at Mercy Hospital, Rockville Centre, New York. He also reviews annulment cases for the Marriage Tribunal of the Archdiocese of New York. Dr. Santos is a member of the Sexual Abuse Review Board for the Prelature of the Holy Cross and Opus Dei and also is a member of the Catholic Medical Association, CatholicTherapists.com, and the Society of Catholic Social Scientists.

The Santoses designed and taught a pre-Cana marriage preparation course, and they write a monthly marriage advice column on CatholicMom.com called "Marriage Rx." They contribute to *FAITH* magazine's "Marriage Matters" advice column. The couple lives in Garden City, New York, with their six children.

AVE
AVE MARIA PRESS

Founded in 1865, Ave Maria Press,
a ministry of the Congregation of
Holy Cross, is a Catholic publishing
company that serves the spiritual and
formative needs of the Church and its
schools, institutions, and ministers;
Christian individuals and families; and
others seeking spiritual nourishment.

For a complete listing of titles from

Ave Maria Press

Sorin Books

Forest of Peace

Christian Classics

visit www.avemariapress.com

AVE MARIA PRESS
Notre Dame, IN
A Ministry of the United States Province of Holy Cross